The

List

100 WAYS
to
SHAKE UP
YOUR
LIFE

GAIL
BELSKY

SEAL PRESS

The List
100 Ways to Shake Up Your Life
Copyright © 2008 by Gail Belsky

Published by
Seal Press
A Member of Perseus Books Group
1700 Fourth Street
Berkeley, California

Library of Congress Cataloging-in-Publication Data

Belsky, Gail.
  The list : 100 ways to shake up your life / by Gail Belsky.
      p. cm.
   ISBN-13: 978-1-58005-256-6
   ISBN-10: 1-58005-256-8
   1. Middle-aged women--Conduct of life. 2. Self-realization in women.
I. Title.
   HQ1059.4.B455 2008
   646.70082--dc22
                         2008020826

Cover design by Gerilyn Attebery
Interior design by Megan Cooney
Illustration by Tim McGrath
Printed in the United States of America by Edwards Bros.
Distributed by Publishers Group West

Credits
Marilyn Meyer poem, "Morning After Dinner with Charlie" was published on the side of Seattle's public busses in 2001, as part of an aptly titled program, "King County Poetry and Art on Busses," and is published by permission of its author.

To Julian, Madeline, and William

INTRODUCTION...16

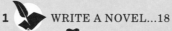

1 WRITE A NOVEL...18

2 DO A TRIATHLON...20

3 STRIP...22

4 CATCH A BIG FISH...24

5 LEARN A FOREIGN LANGUAGE...26

6 WITNESS CHILDBIRTH...28

7 JOIN AN AMBULANCE CREW...30

8 LEARN TO SURF...32

9 AUDITION FOR SOMETHING NERVE-RACKING...34

10 JOIN A RELIEF EFFORT...36

11 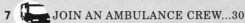 GET A TATTOO (OR A PIERCING)...38

12 ENTER A POKER TOURNAMENT...40

13 RUN FOR OFFICE...42

14 BREW YOUR OWN BEER...44

15 DO A POLAR BEAR SWIM...46

16 DRASTICALLY CHANGE YOUR HAIRSTYLE...48

17 BAKE A WEDDING CAKE...50

18 GO HORSEBACK RIDING, BAREBACK-STYLE...52

19 LAUNCH YOUR OWN WEBSITE...54

20 JOIN A CATTLE DRIVE...56

TABLE
of
CONTENTS

21 BUILD YOUR OWN PIECE OF FURNITURE...58

22 ORGANIZE A RALLY...60

23 GET HYPNOTIZED...62

24 LEARN TRAPEZE...64

25 GO COMMANDO...66

26 VISIT AN ASHRAM...68

27 SHOOT A GUN...70

28 RECORD YOUR OWN MUSIC...72

29 BUY YOURSELF A SEX TOY...74

30 TAKE A LOVER...76

31 HIKE MACHU PICCHU...78

32 HAVE NUDE PICTURES TAKEN...80

33 HAVE A COSMETIC SURGERY PROCEDURE...82

34 DRIVE OVER 100 MILES PER HOUR...84

35 LEARN AN EXOTIC DANCE...86

36 SWIM WITH SEA CREATURES...88

37 DIVE OFF A CLIFF...90

38 SNEAK BACKSTAGE...92

39 SPELUNK...94

40 CREATE A SACRED SPACE...96

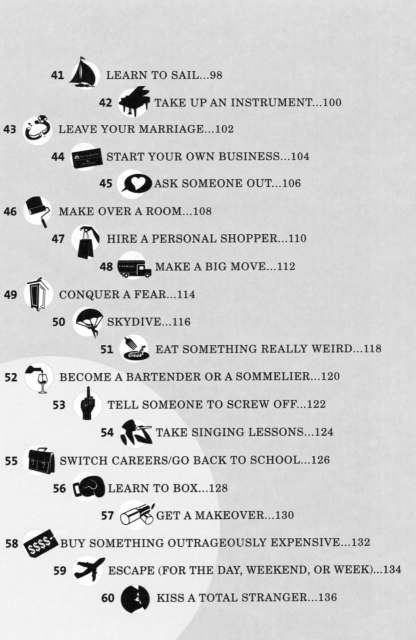

41 LEARN TO SAIL...98

42 TAKE UP AN INSTRUMENT...100

43 LEAVE YOUR MARRIAGE...102

44 START YOUR OWN BUSINESS...104

45 ASK SOMEONE OUT...106

46 MAKE OVER A ROOM...108

47 HIRE A PERSONAL SHOPPER...110

48 MAKE A BIG MOVE...112

49 CONQUER A FEAR...114

50 SKYDIVE...116

51 EAT SOMETHING REALLY WEIRD...118

52 BECOME A BARTENDER OR A SOMMELIER...120

53 TELL SOMEONE TO SCREW OFF...122

54 TAKE SINGING LESSONS...124

55 SWITCH CAREERS/GO BACK TO SCHOOL...126

56 LEARN TO BOX...128

57 GET A MAKEOVER...130

58 BUY SOMETHING OUTRAGEOUSLY EXPENSIVE...132

59 ESCAPE (FOR THE DAY, WEEKEND, OR WEEK)...134

60 KISS A TOTAL STRANGER...136

61  BIKE ACROSS AMERICA...138

62 PLAY IN THE SNOW...140

63 RIDE IN A FIRE TRUCK...142

64 WATCH PORN...144

65 SKINNY-DIP...146

66 BREAK A LONG-HELD TRADITION...148

67 JOIN THE PEACE CORPS...150

68 PLAN A GIRLS' VACATION...152

69 LEARN SURVIVAL SKILLS...154

70 PAINT YOUR HOUSE A WILD COLOR...156

71 TRY HIGH-STAKES GAMBLING...158

72 PLAY ICE HOCKEY...160

73 THROW AN ALL-GIRLS PARTY...162

74 MAKE A SEX TAPE...164

75 LEARN TO DRIVE...166

76 LIE ABOUT SOMETHING...168

77 GO TOPLESS...170

78 SCUBA DIVE...172

79 GET A BRAZILIAN WAX...174

80 USE FOOD AS FOREPLAY...176

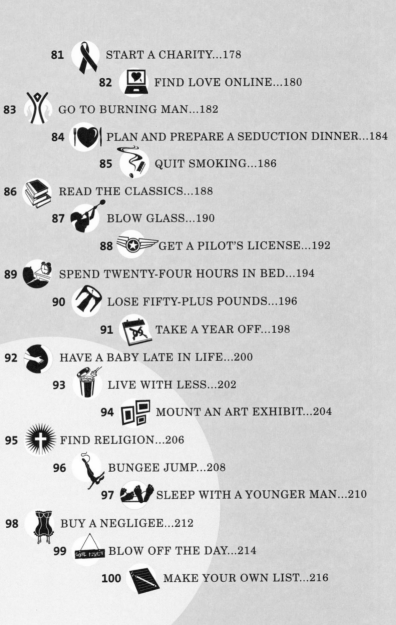

81 START A CHARITY...178

82 FIND LOVE ONLINE...180

83 GO TO BURNING MAN...182

84 PLAN AND PREPARE A SEDUCTION DINNER...184

85 QUIT SMOKING...186

86 READ THE CLASSICS...188

87 BLOW GLASS...190

88 GET A PILOT'S LICENSE...192

89 SPEND TWENTY-FOUR HOURS IN BED...194

90 LOSE FIFTY-PLUS POUNDS...196

91 TAKE A YEAR OFF...198

92 HAVE A BABY LATE IN LIFE...200

93 LIVE WITH LESS...202

94 MOUNT AN ART EXHIBIT...204

95 FIND RELIGION...206

96 BUNGEE JUMP...208

97 SLEEP WITH A YOUNGER MAN...210

98 BUY A NEGLIGEE...212

99 BLOW OFF THE DAY...214

100 MAKE YOUR OWN LIST...216

INTRODUCTION

I rarely step outside of my comfort zone, so writing a book about shaking things up was a voyeuristic thrill for me. Skydiving, starting a charity, sleeping with a much younger man . . . these are things I never consider. I have to sedate myself just to fly in a jet with a seat belt on; the idea of my going up in a dinky little plane and jumping out with a parachute is pretty hysterical. There aren't enough pills in the world.

But that's what stepping outside of your comfort zone is—doing things that are exciting or challenging, even if the mere thought of them makes you sweat bullets. It's about going skydiving *because* you're afraid, not in spite, of it. I learned this from the eighty-two women I interviewed for *The List* who've pushed past their fears and beyond their expectations to do all kinds of cool things—including Jan St. John, who watched her children jump from the plane before she did.

Every time I spoke to one of these women, I felt totally lame— and truly inspired. Hearing how flamenco dance lessons changed Julie Tilsner's life made me want to pick up a pair of castanets for myself, and for every woman I know. When you read these stories, you can't help but be inspired—if not to dance, then to dive off a cliff. Or bake a wedding cake. Or strip. Or do whatever's been languishing on your to-try list for years. You'll love the women of *The List* because they're just like you, except that they've already gotten a Brazilian wax or taken surfing lessons, and you haven't. Not yet.

Not all the shake-ups on *The List* are going to capture your fancy. Just because Anna Melillo went to Burning Man and slept in a converted prison bus for a week doesn't mean you'd entertain the notion for a nanosecond. But reading about the amazing art installations and incredible sense of community she found there might send you off in search of your own enriching experience.

I made a hundred plans while writing *The List*. When I got off the phone with Peg Krygowski after hearing about her cross-country bike trip with her daughter, I rushed to tell my own fifteen-year-old daughter, Madeline, all about it. After talking to Jan St. John about cliff diving in Costa Rica with her grown daughter, I implored Madeline to still want to go away with me when she's grown up. And after talking to M. J. Miller about swimming with manatees in Florida, I screamed upstairs to tell Madeline that I'd found our destination and made her come down and see how cute those manatees looked online. (My son, William, wasn't too thrilled about being left out of the plans, but I'll happily do something special with him, too.)

Manatees with Madeline is on my list now. Here are some other things I hope to get around to doing in the not-too-distant future:

- Sit on the board of a nonprofit organization
- Take William to Venice
- Learn to dive off a diving board
- Take dance lessons

Some of the women I interviewed even told me they had their own list drawn up and were crossing things off as they did them. Sometimes we need to put things on paper to remember how truly important they are.

WRITE A NOVEL

To Do! my own life!

If you were one of those girls who spent the whole of junior high with her head in a book, you might still harbor a dream of writing your own novel. Perhaps you sit in book club every month picking apart the selection and secretly thinking, *Why didn't I try becoming a writer?*

The better question is, why not try now? Many famous novelists have gotten off to a late start. Laura Ingalls Wilder published her first book, *Little House in the Big Woods,* in 1932, at age sixty-five. Harriet Doerr was seventy-four when her first book, *Stones for Ibarra,* won a National Book Award in 1984.

Rachel Cline of New York City started writing her first novel, *What to Keep,* when she was forty-one and had it published in 2004 at age forty-seven. It was her lifelong dream come true. "I had wanted to be a published writer since I was ten," says Cline. "When I turned forty I thought, *If I want to write a book, I'd better start, because nobody's going to ask me to do it.* Now I can say I am a fiction writer."

Selling a book requires a great deal of luck, but writing one simply takes guts. It's not easy to let go of your insecurities, especially since you've been living with them for two or three decades. But how powerful would you feel if you beat back your fears and actually did the thing? Think about it: Right now, the biggest difference between you and the accomplished novelists mentioned above is that they sat down and committed themselves to writing.

Are you ready to get started? Here's what you need to do:

First, think about how you like to work. Novel writing moves at two basic speeds: fast and furious, or slow and steady. If you enjoy working on an extreme deadline—or if you're afraid you'd wimp out if you don't—look into National Novel Writing Month (www.NaNoWriMo.org). This virtual speed-writing program has you starting to write on November 1 and finishing a 175-page, fifty-thousand-word novel by midnight on November 30.

If playing Beat the Clock when you work makes you frantic, rather than focused, try a more methodical approach. Writing coach Alice Elliott Dark, author of the novel *Think of England* and two collections of short stories, lays out this step-by-step plan:

- Pick a genre and choose five novels that belong to it.
- Examine how they are put together. Outline each scene. What happens in each one? How does it advance the story? What's the conflict?
- Read books about writing. Focus on learning about how the plot comes out of the characters. Create your characters and know what type of people they are, and your plot will unfold.
- Look at your schedule. When are you going to work on your book? Be realistic, too, about how long it takes to become a good writer. No one expects to learn to play the violin in six months, so don't be surprised if it takes you longer to write your book than you thought it would.
- Get going and don't look back—not until you've gotten through a first draft. If you revise your work every step of the way, you may never actually arrive at the end. Be playful. Love your characters. Use your imagination. Have fun!

1. WRITE A NOVEL

2

DO A TRIATHLON

For those of us who are so busy that our primary form of exercise is a sprint through the supermarket, the idea of doing a triathlon can be tantalizing—pounding feet, racing heart, the sheer exhilaration of forward motion. What makes this running/biking/swimming competition so compelling is the same thing that makes it so scary: the level of commitment it requires. It's not like skiing, whereby you can go once or twice a year without any training leading up to it. To be a triathlete, you've got to train for sixty to ninety minutes a few times a week for a couple of months. Once you get into it, though, you'll have an enormous sense of accomplishment as you carry yourself forward to the day of your actual event.

My friend Patty, a longtime runner, upped the ante for herself when she entered the 2007 Danskin Triathlon in Sandy Hook, New Jersey, one of fifty women's-only races held in the United States each year. Competing for the first time at age forty-eight, she never expected to finish. But halfway through the competition, she realized she was doing it: "I was passing people. I thought, *I'm actually enjoying myself. I'm going to do it in decent time. And I'm having fun.*"

Because Patty already ran a few times a week, ramping up for the triathlon was relatively simple; she just built on what was already there. But if you've never done much running, or if you've let it slide for a while, you'll need to work on that first. Sounds obvious, but start with a good pair of running shoes. Many factors determine which shoe is best for you: how tall you are, where you'll be running, how high your arch is. Go to a specialty store, and have someone knowledgeable help you choose the right shoe.

Before you raise your foot to run, be sure to lower your expectations. Even if you've run before, if you push yourself too fast, you'll likely get discouraged and quit. Set a modest goal for your first outing—ten minutes if you're a novice, fifteen if you're getting back into it—but if it gets too difficult before then, stop and walk awhile. With subsequent runs, increase your time slowly until you can run comfortably for thirty to forty minutes. At that point, you're ready to start triathlon training. The question is, how do you want to do it?

Some women happily train alone; others need buddies to keep them motivated. Patty never would have competed in the Danskin race if her three regular running mates hadn't signed up, too. Making a commitment to one another made it easier for them to stick to their three-month training regimen. They started with their normal running schedule—forty-five minutes, three times a week—then worked in the other triathlon components: swimming and cycling. They'd meet at the community pool at five forty-five, run three to four miles, and return at six thirty for the "commuter swim." On Saturday mornings they'd go on women's bike rides organized by their local bike shop.

For Patty, who has two children and a full-time job, the rigorous training paid off in more ways than one. "It was a totally selfish thing," she says. "Whatever was going on Saturday mornings, I wasn't available, so everyone else had to deal. I decided that this is what matters to me right now."

3

STRIP

If it's true that sexy is as sexy does, stripping should do it for you like no black lace thong ever could. That's because feeling sexy and looking sexy are two different things. You may think that bumping and grinding and tossing your panties is something you do to please others, but the person who's supposed to be turned on by your show is actually you. How refreshing is that?

If you're not happy with your body or are embarrassed to show it off, stripping can be one of the most liberating things you can do. Imagine being naked, dancing, happy to flaunt your body, despite its flaws. Imagine being a sexy beast—and loving every minute of it.

Deb Kovak took her first exotic-dance class at age forty-eight, after her nineteen-year marriage ended and she became an empty-nester. "When is it ever about you? Well, this is all about me," she says. "It's an awakening to realize that you have to love yourself. It's the sense of freedom . . . of giving yourself permission to let go. It's so empowering to feel good about yourself."

Unless you're living among the mountain goats, chances are good that an exotic-dance class is offered within driving distance of your home. Stripping and pole dancing have become a nationwide fad, with classes popping up in studios and gyms everywhere. You don't need to take a class; there are plenty of how-to DVDs you can rent or buy to teach yourself at home. But there's something comforting, not to mention fun, about letting loose in a room full of women. Until class begins, here are a few ideas to get you started, courtesy of Wendy Reardon, author of *The Complete Idiot's Guide to Exotic and Pole Dancing* and the owner of the Gypsy Rose exotic- and pole-dancing studio in Quincy, Massachusetts.

- Choose a song that makes you feel sexy. Then choose an outfit—something you can peel down, not up over your head.

- Turn on the music and walk into the room very slowly. Step, step, pause, pause. Caress your body lightly with one finger as you go.

- Gently lower yourself to a squat, hands on your knees for balance. Get down onto the floor, one knee at a time. Stick out your butt, and rotate it in circles. Roll your neck for drama.

- Stand up with your butt first and stick it out as far as it will go. Draw your arms up your thighs. Keep stroking yourself lightly. If there's a part of your body you don't like, act like you love it.

- Do a sexy walk over to a wall. Turn around and, with your back against the wall, start sliding down. Slide your hands down your body as you move down the wall.

- Crawl to your partner, rolling your neck. Stand up again, butt first, and undo your costume. Slide the sleeve or strap down one arm and then the other. Slowly peel your outfit down your body to the floor.

- Turn away from your partner. Lean over and bring the costume down to your knees. Then let it fall to the floor and step out of it with one foot.

- Take your clothing and toss it over your shoulder, but don't turn around just yet. Back up slowly and sit on your partner's lap. Take his or her hands and put them on your boobs. Now turn around and do what you want to do, but never forget that this is for you.

4

CATCH A BIG FISH

As a society, we're not very good at sitting around. We like action, decision, results. That's probably why so many sayings exist to mollify us when we do have to bide our time: "Patient as a saint." "Patience is a virtue." "Good things come to those who wait." But if you've ever spent twelve hours in the middle of the ocean with a fishing rod and a pack of antinausea gum, you know those platitudes don't always help.

Of all the hobbies you can take up, fishing has the lowest patience-to-payoff ratio. When you make a model airplane, it may take you six months to finish, but at least you have an impressive Cessna 172 Skyhawk to show for your time. If the fish aren't biting, you can sit there forever and come home with nothing. However, for real enthusiasts, waiting isn't a problem. The longer it takes to catch the big one, the sweeter it is when you do.

Many anglers have fishing in their blood, and their love of the sport runs deep. Like Kathleen Curran, they were raised with a pole in one hand and bait in the other. Curran, who's fifty-eight, started fishing with her father when she was four and vividly remembers his hauling her out of bed one night to see a thirty-five-pound striped bass he'd caught. They would get up at three in the morning to fish in the Hudson River, near the Statue of Liberty, in their little aluminum boat—just the two of them and their own private statue.

When Curran was thirteen, her father wanted to go catch a shark, so she and her brother went out with him and chummed, tossing pig's blood and fish parts into the water to attract the shark. "Sure enough, we got a hit; we were using half a bluefish as bait," she says. "I turned the wheel and it wouldn't go. The shark played for a little while and then let go. The hook was bent sideways—the shark was that big."

That was the one that got away.

It took forty-three more years, but in 2006, Curran finally caught the big one.

While vacationing at an eco-camp on the Baja California peninsula, Curran hired a local fisherman to take her out for the day in his skiff. Carrying a hat and a cooler of sandwiches and cold beers, she met him at his boat at dawn. For the first few hours, she fished for bait. Eventually, she caught a yellowfin tuna. Then they headed out to the middle of the Sea of Cortez. Curran took the last piece of live bait, put it on a hook, and let it go.

"Within seconds, up jumps this beautiful dorado," she says. "I had to play that fish to get him in. It was an epic battle. The fisherman never saw a woman do this. The dorado was four and a half feet long. It was huge, with a head like a dolphin. It was every color . . . like a rainbow. Right before it died, it just glittered."

Curran cried. That day, May 28, was the anniversary of her father's death. "I just felt like it was his spirit," she says.

Curran returned to shore after eight hours on the water. The hired fishermen usually clean the fish, but she took care of this one herself. She cleaned it, filleted it, packaged it up, and gave it to friends. "It's a very personal thing," she says. "I'm always mindful. It's really a spiritual link you have with the creature—you took his life. It didn't even dawn on me until the fish was in the boat what day it was."

Done

LEARN A FOREIGN LANGUAGE

Just before I started writing this book, I planned a trip to Paris with my children—something I swore I wouldn't do until I had learned to speak some French. In 1985 I spent a week in that stunning city, wandering the streets on my own while the friend I was staying with was at work. Without knowing the language, I was virtually mute and totally incompetent. I couldn't even read a menu, so every day I ordered *croque monsieur* for lunch by pointing to it. Pathetic.

I never got around to taking French lessons, and if luck (or fate) hadn't intervened, I would have returned to Paris after two decades with nothing to say for myself. But while I was doing research to prepare for writing this *List* item, I uncovered an incredible opportunity: The Alliance Française in New York had just started holding classes in my town in New Jersey—half a mile from my house. I could *walk* there, for God's sake. So I signed up for the eleven-week beginners' course and began the next week.

On the first day of class, I was surprised by how nervous I felt. (I had visions of myself on the first day of middle school, waiting for the bus in my Quiana dress and platform shoes.) What was there to worry about? I had breezed through Spanish in school and was fairly fluent by the time I got to college. Surely, in three months, I could figure out how to ask for *potage* or *fromage* without humiliating myself.

Or not.

Clearly, I lacked confidence. Maybe it wouldn't come so easily this time. Maybe I wouldn't be able to make the sounds, grasp the sentence structures, or remember the verb conjugations as easily as I had in seventh grade. When I first talked about doing this book, my friend Pam told me that she thinks the older we get, the less we think of ourselves as learners. That didn't resonate with me . . . not until I stood in the doorway of a classroom at St. James Church, clutching my new notebook and pen.

AN ALLIANCE NEAR YOU

Believe it or not, there are more than one hundred independent chapters of the Alliance Française throughout the United States—including five in New Jersey, eight in Texas, and fifteen in California. That's not the only place to get your croissant buttered, however. Colleges, junior colleges, and community schools also teach adult education classes in French and other languages, and the web offers many options. I particularly like the British Broadcasting Company's program at www.bbc.co.uk/languages/french.

Class was hard and confusing. I wasn't as quick as I should have been, and I'm sure nerves had a lot to do with it. But I walked out of there feeling excited—and really pleased with myself. My daughter, Madeline, a strong French student in tenth grade, helped me with my homework, and my twelve-year-old novice, William, drilled me on the alphabet. They thought it was hilarious.

I dropped out of the course early to focus on my book deadlines, and I didn't learn as much as I had hoped to. But when I came back from Paris, I was thrilled to find that I wasn't half the nincompoop I was two decades ago. I could handle the most important dialogue: "Hello. I don't speak French. Do you speak English?" I could also read signs and menus and could pronounce the words somewhat intelligibly, which meant that I didn't have to point at my *brioche sucre* at the *boulangerie* in order to eat breakfast.

6
WITNESS _done_ CHILDBIRTH

There's a wild book called *Spiritual Midwifery*—written by Ina May Gaskin, the mother of all midwives—that I used to give out to my pregnant friends. Gaskin delivered babies on a large Tennessee commune that she and her husband formed in 1971, called The Farm, and has attended more than twelve hundred births since then.

The first half of the book provides case histories (with graphic descriptions and hippie-dippie lingo) of births on the commune. Men sit behind their laboring partners and rub the women's nipples to bring on contractions (or "rushes," as they're called in the book); in turn, the laboring women bellow like moose to deal with the pain. It's a fun read and an excellent guide to the childbirth process.

The second half of the book includes explicit instructions on delivering babies. Reading it during my first pregnancy, I was riveted by the mechanics of childbirth and devoured the entire manual. I learned about rotating shoulders, turning around breeches, and loosening umbilical cords wrapped around babies' necks. Put me in a taxi with a woman in labor, and I'd have that baby out in no time.

Books aren't real life, though, and when I had the chance, years later, to witness the miracle of birth, I was a big, fat chicken about it.

When my sister Judy had her first child in 2001, she invited our older sister Lauren to attend. Lauren spent the entire time at Judy's feet, literally jumping up and down as our nephew came out, saying, "This is the best thing you ever did for me!" Three years later, Judy invited me to her second birth. I stood up at her head the entire time. When the baby crowned, I took two steps toward the doctor to watch my niece make her debut—an unbelievable experience, even from five feet away. Still, I wish I'd been brave enough to get closer, because I may never have another chance to be part of something so magical.

STUCK IN A CAB?
A HANDY GUIDE TO BABY DELIVERY

- Find something to cover the baby, like a towel, blanket, or shirt.
- Birth is imminent when you can see the head crowning. Put your hand in front of the baby's head as it comes out.
- The baby will turn to one side. Gently guide the shoulders as they come out; the body will slip out after them.
- Put the baby on top of the mother, cover it, and rub it.
- If the baby doesn't cry after thirty seconds, pick it up and gently blow two puffs of air into the nose and mouth.
- Don't cut the cord. Go straight to the hospital.

Kriss Kovach, a forty-two-year-old lactation consultant, has attended many births. "It seems both run-of-the-mill and absolutely ridiculous. There's the gut-churning anticipation of seeing another person's head lodged into an impossibly tight spot and wondering if they are going to breathe. The baby seems to glow and bring warmth into the room. It's like kryptonite: not much mass, but a lot of energy."

Laurie Bleich, a fifty-four-year-old midwife, should be jaded by now, but she's still awed by the magnitude of childbirth. "It's life-changing," she says. "It's just exciting to be at a birth, and then you go home. I almost look at people differently. People are always having life changes, and you never know anything about them, but here I was, a witness to one."

If you're lucky, somebody close to you will invite you to witness a birth. You might even get to participate. To watch one human being emerge from another—ten fingers, ten toes, and perfect—is an indescribable experience. One last push, and another person's joined the party.

JOIN AN AMBULANCE CREW

Very few activities allow you to catch a thrill while giving back to your community, but riding with an ambulance crew is a two-for-the-price-of-one deal. Jumping on an emergency vehicle and racing around with the sirens blaring isn't boring. (Slide over, Randolph Mantooth.) Nor is wondering what awaits you at the end of the ride.

The community-service aspect of ambulance work is gratifying in a different way. Unlike many other forms of volunteerism, joining the crew allows you to offer immediate help to people in need. You're there on the spot during a crisis, so there's no doubt in your mind that what you're doing is making a real difference.

That's what compelled Laurie Alberts to join her local crew after she turned fifty. "A kind of a restlessness came over me," she says. "It got to a point where I wondered if anything I did had any meaning at all. I needed to do something that was immediately useful."

Rescue work was a logical choice for a woman who was a big *Rescue 911* fan in the '90s. "I used to get really excited by it," Alberts says. "It was just a fascination, but someone else might call it ghoulishness." She had always been a thrill seeker (at least, until marriage and mother-hood took center stage), and emergency rescue definitely fit the bill.

"I was working on a part of my personality that I had put aside for a while. I'm so set in my ways that nothing ever changes," says Albert. "This satisfied my need to put myself out there in a different way."

If you think riding on an ambulance crew could do the same for you, you'll need to complete a training and certification process for emergency medical technicians (EMTs). Community colleges, some state colleges, and hospitals all offer courses, which usually run three months. The National Registry of Emergency Medical Technicians certifies emergency medical service providers at thee different levels: EMT-Basic, EMT-Intermediate, and EMT-Paramedic. Here's what you'd be handling on the job:

EMT-Basic: bleeding, fractures, airway obstruction, cardiac arrest, and emergency childbirth, plus common emergency equipment, such as backboards, suction devices, splints, oxygen-delivery machines.

EMT-Intermediate: all of the above, plus advanced airway devices, intravenous fluids, and some medications. Varies by state.

EMT-Paramedic: all of the above, plus drugs (both oral and intravenous), electrocardiograms (EKGs), endotracheal intubations, monitors, and other complex equipment. Varies by state.

Depending on where you live, you could even turn emergency-response work into a new career. There's no shortage of jobs in this field; in fact, the demand for EMTs is expected to grow by 19 percent between 2006 and 2016. By that time, an estimated 240,000 EMTs will be certified, which isn't bad, considering that the U.S. didn't even have an EMT or paramedic program until the early 1970s—right around the time that Mantooth raced to his first emergency on Squad 51.

SO YOU WANT TO BE AN EMT

- Average salary: $39,000 for government employees, $30,000 for hospital employees, and $32,000 for private companies
- Average hours: fifty hours per week for fire department employees, forty-five to sixty hours per week for hospital employees, and forty-five to fifty hours for private ambulance employees
- Job prospects: good, particularly in cities and for private companies
- Requirements: state certification

LEARN TO SURF

During one of our summer vacations on Block Island, Rhode Island, my husband and I took our two children to see a documentary called *Riding Giants* about the legends of big-wave surfing. None of us surfed, and we really couldn't have cared less about the sport, but there were only two movie theaters on the island and we'd seen everything else they were showing. I was expecting a real snooze, but the movie was fascinating.

Riding fifty-foot waves seemed to be the recreational equivalent of outrunning a tornado. The physical feats were awesome, but the guys who performed them were even more amazing. They were the classic surfer dudes of the 1950s and '60s—sinewy, suntanned boys who lived in tents on the beaches of Hawaii, spearing fish for dinner and surfing killer waves all day long. While Jack Kerouac was riding around in cars, these renegades were hanging ten. They were more than counterculture— they were surf culture.

I can't tell you exactly what that means, but Elise Cannon can. She grew up in a surfing town in California. Her brothers surfed—all the boys did. She can think of only two girls who rode the waves, and they were considered tomboys. "I loved the ocean, but I deselected myself from surfing early on," says Cannon, who's forty-six. "I always felt it was a culture I didn't belong to; it was beautiful boys who did this." (That is, white boys whose parents weren't strict and let them go to the beach often). As mellow as most of the guys were, they formed a "locals only" clique that was hard to break into.

COOL CAMPS FOR SURFER CHICKS

- Saltwater Cowgirls, Jacksonville Beach, Florida
- Las Olas Surf Safaris for Women, Pacific Mexico
- Surf Diva, San Diego, California
- Maui Surfer Girls, Maui, Hawaii
- Venus Surf Adventures, Rio Claro de Pavones, Costa Rica

In college, Cannon had a boyfriend who took her out once on a longboard. The surf was heavy, and she didn't have the skill or the strength to paddle out far enough to catch a wave. Exhausted, she gave up. "After that, I would sit on the shore and take pictures, waiting there for him with a drink," she says. "It was just too daunting."

Cannon didn't try again for twenty years, but she realized that she didn't want to give up on it altogether. "It was always this thing I had yearned for but was afraid to try," she says. As she approached forty, Cannon saw a brochure for a one-week women's surf camp near Puerto Vallarta. "I knew I didn't want to spend my birthday in town," she recalls. "I got a cheap ticket for $300, and next thing I knew I was on an airplane, heading to surf camp."

The first thing the campers worked on was their pop-up—how to stand up on their board as they are catching a wave. Instead of taking the waves head-on, they learned how to paddle around them and glide into them. Cannon caught a wave her first time out. "It was incredible," she says. "I grabbed the hand of a strange guy who was surfing next to me. It was very exciting; people were cheering." It made a big difference for Cannon to be able to learn with—and be taught by—a group of women. "They knew how to make it fun on the first day. It was non-threatening. You didn't have to break into the culture."

The lesson here: Don't count yourself out . . . of anything.

AUDITION FOR SOMETHING NERVE-RACKING

When you were a kid and adults asked you what you wanted to be when you grew up, did you tell them you planned to become a molecular biologist, or did you tell them the truth: "I wanna be a rock star/actress/ballerina"? We're not likely to get cornered at parties by people asking us what our dream job would be, but if somebody did ask, what would you say?

It's okay to admit that you've still got stage lust. The lure of the limelight rarely fades, even after you've become a landscape designer and mother—or grandmother. No matter what else you've done, the performer in you will always want to perform. The question is, will you let her try?

The prospect of auditioning and putting your talent on the line for others to judge may be as scary now as it was when you were eleven. But for many women, the feeling that it's "now or never" overrides the jitters. Really, what do you have to lose, other than more time?

> **"You're giving a performance, not taking a test. You can get up and give a performance!"**
> —Kathryn Joosten, age 68

Kathryn Joosten vowed in her twenties not to let time slide, after watching her mother die of cancer. "My mother died young and angry because she had put off many of her dreams," she says. "I realized there wasn't going to be a 'later.' I was so impressed by the bitterness that she had." When Joosten was divorced at forty-two and struggling to raise two boys on her own, she decided there was no better time to try her hand at acting.

"My first career was as a nurse, for nine years. Then I married the doctor . . . and ten years later I was on my own," Joosten says. "I now had the rest of my life to deal with; the plan I originally had just went out the window."

So she started creating a new one. Her local theater group was holding auditions for a production of *Gypsy* at the time, and Joosten tried out for it. She was uniquely qualified: Her aunt, a former Mafia girlfriend, had taught her the bump-and-grind as a kid. She knew she'd ace the audition the minute she took the stage. "I can't imagine where I got the guts to sing in public. But it was a character, and I knew I could do it. It was a lark—why not?"

To support her acting habit—and her children—Joosten worked three jobs. She was a greeting lady for Royal Welcome, a wallpaper hanger (author Dave Eggers says she did his bedroom when he was a kid), and a location manager for films. But she wanted to take a year to see if she could launch an acting career. "I had a little bit of success in the community theater and managed to get the attention of an agent," she says. "I went to my sons, who were ten and twelve, and said, 'I could get a job in an office, but I would really like to try acting and I need your permission.' I was very lucky; both of them said, 'Go for it.'"

Joosten is sixty-eight now, with one hundred television and movie credits under her belt and an Emmy on her mantelpiece for her recurring role as Karen McCluskey on *Desperate Housewives*.

"You take your life in your hands and you make it happen," she says. "You don't let it happen to you."

JOIN A RELIEF EFFORT

In 1999, when Tropical Storm Floyd hit, the Raritan River in New Jersey flooded, sending twelve feet of water down Main Street in the town of Bound Brook, a.k.a. the Floodiest Town in America. Two people drowned, thousands fled to shelters, homes and businesses were destroyed, and I watched it all on the news from my own (dry) home thirty-three miles away. It would have taken me forty to fifty minutes to drive down there the next day, week, or even month to help with the cleanup effort. Did I go? No.

In 2005, when Hurricane Katrina hit, I was on vacation with my family and didn't even realize what had happened until three days after the fact. When I got home, I pulled out my credit card and donated money to relief efforts. Meanwhile, Lisa Walsh and her friends in Randolph, Massachusetts, were gathering donated clothes, baby wipes, and personal-hygiene products to drive down to a community center in Lafayette, Louisiana.

"I'm in recovery. There's a bunch of women in the group who've been running together for a long time, and we wanted to do something," says Walsh, who's forty-two.

One of the women placed an ad in the local paper looking for donations, and soon her entire front lawn was covered with large garbage bags filled with supplies. "It blew up," says Walsh. "People were just dying to do something, and nobody knew what to do in those first weeks."

In addition to being in recovery together, Walsh and her friends are bikers (the name of their AA group is In the Wind). A number of them owned trailers for hauling motorcycles, but since Walsh and her husband are self-employed, they volunteered to make the drive. When they pulled out of town, there wasn't an inch of space left in their cargo camper. And when they pulled into Lafayette two days later, they could barely comprehend what they had seen.

"These communities were ghost towns," Walsh says. "You could see the water lines on the buildings. Everything was debris: abandoned cars, lawn mowers, kids' toys. Community after community—bedroom communities, housing projects—the hurricane didn't discriminate. It took the Mercedes down and the crappy, beat-up Chevys down.

"Imagine walking up your street and seeing your house and your neighbor's house underwater, and all your stuff floating around. You just can't wrap your mind around that kind of event.

"Used clothes were probably the least of these people's needs. Nobody had any idea what they had really lost; they lost what they had worked for their whole lives, what their parents had worked for their whole lives. And we go down with a couple of baby wipes and T-shirts we don't wear anymore.

"We wanted to do the right thing, and in essence it was the right thing. But it was such a small part. It definitely made me feel like there's more to do out there, more than just what you do in your small community."

GET A TATTOO
(OR A PIERCING) Done

Women react to other women's tattoos in one of two basic ways: They're either intrigued or repulsed. In either case, they've certainly been looking, which is exactly the point for many tattoo wearers. A butterfly or crossbones design is sure to be eye-catching and, more important, to make an impression. If you've been feeling like you've faded into the woodwork, an artistic statement on your ankle, shoulder, or forearm—wherever—will give you the presence you've been missing. Here's what else a tattoo can do for you:

- Allow you to reveal something of yourself that you might not be able to express in any other way.
- Help mark something important in your life—a lover, a dream, a birth, or even a loss—with a permanent tribute.
- Keep you feeling young, particularly in the face of a milestone birthday—forty, fifty, sixty, seventy—that makes you want to scream out, "So what? I can still do this if I want to!"

For Angela Pino, it was all of the above—plus a chance encounter with a tattooed motorcycle mama at the dry cleaner—that led her to Big Joe's (no joke) tattoo parlor in 2002. Pino had debated getting a tattoo since her twenties, but her inhibitions had always held her back—having a tattoo just didn't match people's perceptions of her. Then, two months after Pino's birthday, her sister Marianne was diagnosed with advanced intestinal cancer, and Pino stopped caring what other people thought.

THE PIERCING ADVANTAGE

While it doesn't afford you the same kind of artistic expressiveness as a tattoo, piercing is a less permanent way to make your statement. If you grow tired of having a serpent—or the name of your ex-lover—on your collarbone, you'll pay dearly to have it removed (more than ten times what you paid for it in the first place). But if you fall out of love with your navel ring or nose stud, you can just take it out.

"The diagnosis brought it back into focus again," she says. "I was going to do what I want to do. I was going to live my life."

Pino had researched tattoo parlors online and visited a few. But once she saw Big Joe's, the motorcycle mama's favorite, her search was over. "I spent two or three afternoons in the place, looking through pictures," she says.

Pino arranged for her sister to accompany her to Big Joe's. Marianne had also toyed with the idea of getting a tattoo, but she couldn't at that point because of her chemo treatments. So she watched Pino get a sunflower on her inner ankle and planned for her own parlor visit when she was cancer-free.

Was it painful? Very. But the pain was more relentless than it was intense, according to Pino. As long as she talked constantly, it was manageable. And worth it. That summer, sporting a bathing suit and her sunflower, Pino felt like a new woman—a confident woman. "I loved it. It made me feel cool," she says. "It let people know there's more to know about me. I'm not just a suburban wife with two kids."

Two years later, after her sister died, Pino returned to Big Joe's to get a second tattoo, this one on her back. Marianne had wanted the Chinese character for victory. Pino got the Chinese character for courage.

ENTER A POKER TOURNAMENT

With most sports, you can either play for fun or play to win. With tournament poker, there's only one way to play. If you've ever questioned your potential for aggressiveness or your lust for victory, join the nearest poker league and pull up a chair. You might not recognize yourself.

Like chess, poker is a game of strategy, so winning comes down to one thing: how good you are. You can learn to play online and continue to hone your skills there, competing against virtual cigar chompers. (Poker is still largely considered to be a man's game.) Or you can move outside your comfort zone and play against real people who will judge you, scrutinize your every move, and try to psych you out. Can you take it? Many women can, and more are joining their ranks all the time.

Poker is the hottest sport to sweep the country since NASCAR. Fifty-four thousand people competed in the 2007 World Series of Poker, which paid out a total of $160 million—including $8 million to the first-prize winner. But the two sports are very different. Racing is for fans; poker is for players. Racing blows your eardrums; poker strains your brain. Racing is about other people's nerves of steel; poker is about yours.

"I don't have any history of playing cards or slot machines," says Connie, age fifty-eight, who began playing Texas Holdem two years ago when she broke her foot and got tired of reading.

After playing online for three months—at sites like Fulltilt.com, Pokerstars.com, and Ultimatebet.com—Connie wanted to move on from "brick-and-mortar games" to "live games." Through word of mouth, she found a free league. She showed up one night, signed up on the spot, and started playing.

"It's very intimidating," she says. "You don't want to embarrass yourself. The players are 85 to 90 percent men, and most are in their twenties. Very few women over forty play, so you don't have many colleagues there. And a lot of the men don't want to play with Grandma; they don't want to beat Grandma."

> ## SPEAKING OF POKER . . . FAMOUS PHRASES, FROM THEIR TABLE TO YOURS
>
> - Ace in the hole
> - Ace up one's sleeve
> - Beats me
> - Blue chip
> - Call someone's bluff
> - Cash in
> - Full tilt
> - High roller
> - Pass the buck
> - Poker face
> - Stack up
> - Up the ante
> - When the chips are down
> - Wild card

In the beginning, Grandma didn't want to beat them, either.

"I was a fearful, tight player because you don't win at this game without being aggressive," Connie says. "You make huge bets that put a lot of pressure on other players. You are an aggressor, and I have discomfort with that. But in the last three months, I've been evolving into a very aggressive player. It's been a surprise to me that I overcame that fear in a relatively short time."

The free leagues play for two months, and the top players move up to larger tournaments. Connie once played in a twelve-hour tournament with 150 competitors. The grand prize included a seat at the World Series in Las Vegas. Connie would love to play there, to be around people who understand her interest in the game and who are interested in poker strategy. She'd also like to win.

ELECT ME

RUN FOR OFFICE

What makes someone want to get into politics? Is it power? Fame? Front-row seats at minor-league sporting events? Or are people lured by the opportunity to effect positive change in their community?

Chances are, it's none of the above—at least not initially. Often people get into politics because someone else thinks they should. Robin Schlager and Kathy Larson were both reluctant candidates, pressed into service by others with a particular agenda. In Schlager's case, a mayoral candidate was trying to fill his slate; with Larson, a neighborhood group was searching for an advocate. Schlager ran and won, Larson ran and lost, and both were very happy with the outcome. Democracy at work.

Schlager and I live in the same town, a suburb of New York City that has nearly forty thousand residents. When the candidate for mayor asked her to run for town council on his ticket, she said no—almost absolutely, definitely not. Her only experience was as president of the parent-teacher association, and she didn't think she was ready for town politics.

Here's what she thought: *I'm not doing this. It involves the two things I hate most: public speaking and being on TV.*

Then the phone calls began. People had heard she might run for town council. She reiterated her position to the would-be mayor: "Thank you. It's very flattering. But I don't want to do this." The candidate called

Schlager's husband and convinced him that she should run. And in the end, her husband convinced her.

The political machine was already humming when she jumped into the race. Schlager was amazed to find twenty or so people working the campaign, including some with experience in national elections. "I ran on a slate with five other people, plus the mayor," she says. "We lived and breathed this election for two months. We raised a lot of money. We had to work on a platform collectively and set goals."

They held meetings and more meetings. In addition to having a regular Saturday-morning strategy session, the candidates met with the heads of the various town departments—sanitation, recreation, and recycling—as well as with the board of education and the superintendent of schools. They went from house to house, ringing doorbells, and on election day, their hard work paid off.

The political handlers disappeared immediately, and suddenly Councilwoman Schlager was on her own. She called the township clerk and asked what would happen if she couldn't do the job. What if she resigned? The answer was simple: The person who had gotten the second-highest number of votes would step in.

"It took me a good year to really digest it . . . for it to sink in that I had a little bit of power," says Schlager. "It was scary."

A natural procrastinator, she had to learn to make informed decisions quickly. She also had to adjust to life as a public figure: "At cocktail parties, people tell me about their garbage, or their leaf pickup. It's changed my social life." Still, Schlager's going back for more—she's campaigning now for re-election. "Politics is very romantic, and it's hard to let go," she says. "It's not the notoriety; it's just very engaging. It's exciting. I didn't graduate from college. That I could go this far is amazing."

14

BREW YOUR OWN BEER

I like wine, and I love *I Love Lucy,* but I would never think of stomping around in a vat of grapes to make my own Merlot. Nor would I wash, soak, and steam ten pounds of short-grain rice to brew my own sake, or peel fifty pounds of potatoes to make my own vodka. Like most women, I just want to open the bottle and enjoy my drink without having to work or wait for it.

There is, however, a small group of women who will work like crazy to brew their own beer. They'll put up with a mess in their kitchens and lingering odors in their houses. They'll spend four to five weeks boiling, fermenting, and bottling to be able to pop the top off their own home brew and foist it on friends and family. Why? Because it's fun and different. And who knows? Maybe it'll taste good.

Lynne Macco, who's fifty, became a brewmeister (mistress?) when her twenty-two-year-old son decided to whip up a few batches of India Pale Ale and Brown in their kitchen. "It was his ploy to get cheap beer," says Macco, who decided to join him. It was easy for them to get started because the owner of their local hardware store brews his own beer and stocks all of the necessary supplies. Beer-making kits and supplies are readily available online, regardless, if it turns out that your hardware store owner actually buys his like the rest of us.

The few times Macco and her son brewed beer together, it was a messy endeavor. "You make five gallons; I know we had forty bottles," she says. "You can't guess how much room there is in the bottle until the beer gets to the top. It invariably spills over, and the house smells like a brewery. I don't think there was too much alcohol, but the taste was there."

WHAT YOU NEED TO GET STARTED

THE EQUIPMENT:
❶ Brewpot: For boiling malt extract, water, and hops ❷ Fermenter: Plastic bucket or pail for holding the beer as it's being fermented ❸ Funnel and Strainer: For transferring the contents of your brew pot into the fermenter ❹ Siphon Hose: For transferring your beer from the fermenter into the empty beer bottles ❺ Airlock and Stopper: Keeps outside air from getting into the fermenter, while letting carbon dioxide out ❻ Thermometer: For measuring the temperature of your brew at different stages ❼ Bottling Bucket: For holding the mixture of the finished beer and the priming solution before bottling ❽ Beer Bottles and Capper: For packaging and storing your finished beer

THE INGREDIENTS:
Malt extract
Hops
Yeast
Water
Sugar (dextrose or glucose) for carbonation

THE STEPS:
❶ Choose a type of beer; ❷ Buy the ingredients and equipment; ❸ Sanitize the equipment (that's a biggie, according to Macco); ❹ Make the wort (the "raw" beer liquid, usually just malted grains and water); ❺ Ferment the beer; ❻ Prime and bottle; ❼ Store your beer

14. BREW YOUR OWN BEER

DO A POLAR BEAR SWIM

The phrase "take the plunge" means to commit to something—particularly something risky. It's a nice way of saying, "Stop wimping out," which is what we tell ourselves when we agonize over doing something we really want to do but are deathly afraid to try. This saying, which, most literally, means to cast oneself into water, is particularly apt if you've ever even entertained the idea of doing a polar bear swim, the New Year's tradition of running headlong into an icy lake or ocean with a herd of insane people.

Talk about ambivalence: You're standing in a racerback in the freezing cold, staring out over frigid water, wondering if it's too late to run back to the car and head to the nearest bar for a hot toddy. Still, just thinking about diving in is exhilarating. You can practically feel the sting of the water on your skin. Once you do go in, it's so cold that you literally stop breathing and your mind goes numb. It's one of the most death-defying challenges you can imagine, short of jumping out of a plane. (See page 116 to learn about that particular plunge.) The excitement may not register while you're in there, but that's okay. The thrill of this type of stunt comes later, when you can marvel—and brag—about having done it.

Ellen Yacoe, fifty-three, has taken the plunge in Delaware four times with her husband and teenage daughter. Each time, she's had to talk herself into it: "Yes, it's scary, but it's not going to kill you." For a born second-guesser like Yacoe, the polar bear swim is a chance to break through her apprehension and just go for it. "It builds confidence," she says. "You know you want to do something, but there's this anxiety behind it. Then you do it, and you can tell the story for the rest of the year."

If you live anywhere near a lake or an ocean, it won't be hard to find a New Year's swim to join. There are polar bear clubs throughout the United States, from Coney Island in New York to Jacksonport, Wisconsin, to Page-Lake Powell, Arizona. Some have swims throughout the winter, if you decide you can't get enough.

For Yacoe, once a year is plenty. She and her family arrive at the beach, wearing sweats and sweaters over their bathing suits, with plenty of time to spare before the 1:00 PM start. Four minutes before the whistle blows, they join a hundred other people trickling down to the water's edge, then strip down to their suits. "You do a little dance to stay warm," Yacoe says, "and you start to think, *How do I look? Did I shave today? I hope not, because the more hair, the better.*" Or maybe you wonder, *Am I crazy?*

At one o'clock sharp, it's a moot point. As the crowd surges toward the sea or the lake, you'll get swept away, half-petrified, half-electrified. "You run in full speed, take a deep breath, scream, go in, dive headfirst, come up, scream again, run back out," says Yacoe. The plunge itself takes two seconds, and when she runs back to the shore, she feels utterly elated.

"It's an awakening; it's so positive and life affirming," she says. "Now the year can start; bring it on. You can walk away knowing you're a polar club member."

And that you've earned that hot toddy.

DRASTICALLY CHANGE YOUR HAIRSTYLE

A woman's preference in hairstyles is a personal thing, but it certainly isn't private. Short of running around in a burlap sack with a face full of clown paint, nothing you can do to your appearance will attract more attention than a change in your 'do—especially a dramatic one. And nothing will elicit more comments from people you know. (When was the last time someone said, "Wow, you changed your shoe style"?)

Hubert Givenchy once said, "Hair style is the final tip-off whether or not a woman really knows herself." When you shock people with a different cut, it can also be a sign that *they* really don't know *you*. Or maybe that's your point.

> **"Violet will be a good color for hair at just about the same time that brunette becomes a good color for flowers."**
>
> —Fran Lebowitz

For whatever reason, how you wear your hair speaks volumes about your state of being and your state of mind. Grow it long, and you're feeling sexy. Chop it off, and you've experienced a major life change. Dye it a wild color, and you're either rebellious or really bored. Shave it off, and you've got something to tell the world.

That was Chryss Yost's intention. Here's her story: "As part of a war protest, artist Erin O'Brien set up a Peace Salon in front of the Santa

Barbara Museum of Art on the Friday before Veterans Day, offering buzz cuts," says Yost, who is forty-one. "My brother is a marine who served in Iraq. I chose to get a buzz cut as a sign of solidarity with him and other soldiers risking their lives, visibly showing the effect the war has on soldiers' families.

"Like most Americans, I support the soldiers and oppose this war. Having a buzz cut hasn't been easy for me. It's been a challenge, especially with my conservative family and holiday celebrations . . . answering over and over that most dreaded question: '*What* did you *do* to your *hair?*'

"It's also raised interesting issues of sexuality for me. I'm a straight woman, with a lot of interaction with gay women, and never thought of myself as someone with 'issues.' Yet I found myself unsettled by the way my haircut seemed to imply something about my sexuality. As my dad so eloquently greeted me, the first time he saw me postbuzz, 'It's my butch daughter!' And much of society seems to agree. Why does this bother me?

"It was also less than a month from my first wedding anniversary, and it had been a rocky first year. There may have been a little spite involved in my doing it, even though my husband said he didn't care if I did it. Sadly, he really *didn't* care. I kept hoping he would.

"I am proud of myself for taking action. Unlike other protests— marches, letters, and gatherings—this is one I display every day. Even now, three months later, I still find myself explaining my hairstyle to someone new every few days."

The reasons for a hairstyle change are myriad. For my oldest friend from college, Beth, who's forty-six, going from red to blond, mid-length to short, in 2002 was a response to changes in the world (September 11) and in herself (hitting middle age). For me, it was a need to see someone new in the mirror (see "Get a Makeover" on page 130).

What's your reason?

BAKE A
WEDDING CAKE

I f you've ever baked a cake, you know it takes the precision of a laser surgeon not to screw it up. A pinch too much flour or too little baking soda can derail even the most reliable of recipes, and even when you do everything right, there are no guarantees. Frequent bakers accept this truth and forge ahead anyway because they enjoy the process, the result, or both.

When you're a baker, you always have something to aspire to: a cake more delicate, difficult, or delicious than you've ever made. Black forest, perhaps, or three-layer coconut-pineapple. But the holy grail of amateur baking is the wedding cake. Imagine the triumph of pulling it off, especially if you're doing it for someone you love.

Finding a recipe won't be hard, but you might want guidance through the actual baking process. YouTube has a how-to video from two chefs (www.youtube.com/watch?v=CBZ1lMrP43g), and Epicurious offers a wedding cake cooking class from *Bon Appétit* (www.epicurious .com/bonappetit/cooking_class/weddingcake).

Still not sure you can do it? Neither was Missy Pentecost. But that didn't stop her from rising to the challenge when a friend from church asked her to make the cake for a wedding she was hosting.

"My first instinct was to say no, of course," says Pentecost, who is forty. "Not only was it the volume, it was somebody's wedding! What if it looked terrible? What if it tasted terrible?" Luckily, the bride wanted something simple: a three-tiered white butter cake with raspberry filling. Two layers per tier. Fondant icing. Ribbons and flowers as decoration.

Pentecost started baking two days before the wedding and froze the layers until the morning of, when she made the raspberry filling and assembled each tier individually. The fondant icing came ready-made in sheets, and Pentecost draped it over each tier, molding it to the shape of the cake. She wrapped ribbons around each layer, laid layer on top of layer using dowels, and inserted flowers into Wilton flower spikes she'd put around the cake.

"I thought it looked beautiful," she says. "I felt really satisfied. That I had been able to pull it off was exciting."

The hostess reported that the cake was divine.

MISSY'S WHITE BUTTER CAKE RECIPE

6 oz. unsalted butter	¾ tsp. cream of tartar
2 cups sugar	1¼ cups milk
1 tsp. salt	¾ tsp. vanilla extract
3⅓ cups cake flour	¾ cup egg whites (6–8 large egg whites)
1½ tsp. baking powder	½ cup sugar

❶ In a large bowl, cream butter, sugar, and salt with an electric mixer until light and fluffy. ❷ Sift together dry ingredients. ❸ Add dry ingredients to butter mixture, alternating with milk and vanilla. ❹ In a separate bowl, beat egg whites until foamy. Continue beating at high speed while gradually adding ½ cup of sugar, until stiff peaks form. ❺ Fold egg whites into batter with rubber spatula, blending just until whites are evenly distributed. ❻ Divide batter between two prepared 10-inch round cake pans. Bake at 350 degrees for 25–30 minutes, or until cake tester inserted into center comes out clean. (Baking time is less for smaller pans.) ❼ Cool in pans on a rack for 15–20 minutes before turning out of pans.

NOTE: This recipe yields nine cups of batter, so you'll need to multiply based on the number and size of the tiers.

17. BAKE A WEDDING CAKE

Done but not bareback

GO HORSEBACK RIDING, BAREBACK-STYLE

Every grade had one: a horse girl who spent half her life at the barn, grooming, riding, and dreaming. In my class, it was my friend Marcia, who grew up in a house full of underage equestrians. She and her two sisters were avid riders; the three of them lived and breathed horses. Marcia rode all the way through junior and senior high school, even after she broke her collarbone in a bad fall and had to wear a sling over her Fair Isle sweaters for two months.

You didn't have to ride horses to fantasize about them; you just had to be a deep and sensitive girl between the ages of eight and fourteen. There was plenty to fuel those fantasies, too: *Misty of Chincoteague*, *Black Beauty*, *National Velvet*, and *Run Wild, Run Free*, starring the dreamy Mark Lester (remember *Oliver*?) as a selective mute from the English moorlands who shuts down around people but bonds with a white colt. Wild horses were particularly exciting—the thought of jumping onto their bare backs and charging through the woods represented the ultimate drama and romance at that age.

And at this age?

If you can still hear the beating of hooves and feel the wind rushing through your hair, why not see what it's *really* like to ride a horse bareback through the forest—or down the beach, or around a riding ring? That's the great thing about being a grownup: You don't have to ask for permission or a ride. You can take yourself there.

If you haven't spent much time in a saddle, you might want to try doing that first. Go to your local stables and sign up for beginner riding lessons. When you've got the basics down and your balance is pretty good, you can try doing it au naturel.

Women who ride bareback say that taking off the saddle is like cutting out the middleman. "You feel the movement of the horse," says Laurie Alberts, who's fifty-five and owns four horses. "It's very rhythmic. It's freer. My interest as a rider is to have good communication with my horse. You feel that kind of closeness. Your legs are right on them."

It takes a bit more doing for Alberts to ride bareback these days than it did when she was twelve. She has to line up her horse along a fence and stand on a stump or a mounting box before she can hop on. But the thrill is still there.

"Riding bareback is more exciting because there's not much to hold on to," she says. "I bounce more because there are no stirrups. I grab the mane for balance. I give a squeeze of my leg. It's better. The horse feels you more."

As free and easy as it seems in your dreams, jumping on a naked horse and riding takes practice—particularly to get the balance down. Alberts recommends taking lessons with an instructor who will let you ride bareback during class time. Meanwhile, here are some tips for a smooth, safe ride:

- Wear a helmet.
- Pick a calm horse with a smooth gait and a wide back.
- Use a mounting block or a leg up to get on.
- Mount from the left side of the horse. Go easy.
- Sit back on your sit bones, and keep your lower legs close to the horse.
- Grab the mane if you need to; it won't hurt the horse.

LAUNCH YOUR OWN WEBSITE

In recent years, technology has gone out of its way to embrace people who don't naturally embrace it—people like me, and perhaps you. I certainly enjoy the wired (and wireless) life: I talk on my cell, watch digital cable, write on my laptop, and spend every waking minute online. But I don't get how these things work, and I don't really want to think too much about it. Technical information overwhelms me.

Still, as a freelance writer, I need to sell myself and my services. Isn't that the point of having a site—to promote your catering/chiropractic/carpet-cleaning business? When my first book came out and I finally decided to move forward, my husband offered to build me a website. He'd created a very serviceable one for himself using templates from a software package.

I would sooner have had him perform a splenectomy on me, so little confidence did I have in his technological abilities. It was a classic case of transference: He wasn't the one who couldn't fathom the process—I was. So I paid a web designer to build my site, as if she had been born knowing this stuff and didn't need to learn it herself.

Today, there are so many websites about building websites that they completely fill four Google pages. Some services are free; other sites charge for various things. All provide templates for you to fill in with words and pictures. On some sites, you can even copy and drag content, photos, and video off the Internet.

Trade associations are another source of free templates. I know a number of writers who've used a simple template offered by the

Authors Guild, which provides complete web services to its members (www.authorsguild.net). Altrue serves nonprofit organizations (www.altrue.com), and Small Farm Central provides services to—you guessed it—small-farm owners (www.smallfarmcentral.com).

ONLINE TOOLS TO HELP YOU

- Atomz.com
- Google Pages
- iWeb
- Sitekreator.com
- Weebly.com
- Wordpress.com

Sometimes you really do need expert help—particularly if you're building something very complicated and very creative, as Adair Lara, age fifty-six, did. Finding someone to help her construct the site was no easy task. "It was incredibly expensive to deal with anybody in the web-designing business," she says. "They were charging $700 just to consult." So she put an ad on Elance.com for freelance web designers to bid on her project. She ended up with a firm in India that charged $10 an hour. For six months, via email, she fed them words and ideas and checked their progress.

Tending to her website has proven much more difficult than launching it, and Lara's been looking for someone in the United States to help manage it. She's gotten zero response. So she's thinking of going overseas again: "This is more like running a business, and I'm not a businessperson. I don't have the obsessiveness and energy it takes. I feel like I put a little child into the world and left it on its own."

At least she gave birth. Some of us are still too chicken to go there.

JOIN A CATTLE DRIVE

Y ou've no doubt heard of Annie Oakley, Calamity Jane, and Dale Evans. How about Connie Reeves? Probably not. Reeves, the oldest member of the Cowgirl Hall of Fame, died a few years ago at the age of 101. Cause of death: heart attack, twelve days after being thrown from her favorite horse.

Her cowgirl spirit lives on in many women, including some who've never patted a real horse on the nose, let alone ridden one. What goes into that special brand of pluck? It's a combination of unbridled optimism, grit, and a lust for adventure. It's what makes you—a regular Jane with a day job and credit card bills—dream of saddling up, riding a horse through some of the most beautiful scenery in the country, and moving a bunch of cows from one place to another.

CATTLE DRIVE ROUNDUP

If going on a cattle drive is your dream, making it come true is easy. Dozens of guest ranches in the mountain states and the Southwest offer all-inclusive drives, at rates ranging from around $150 a night to $2,075 a week. Here are just a few to look into:

- Badger Creek Ranch, Cañon City, Colorado
- Powder River Cattle Drive, Broadus, Montana
- Dryhead Ranch, in the Dryhead region of Montana
- Bar H Bar Ranch, Soda Springs, Idaho
- Burnt Well Guest Ranch, Roswell, New Mexico
- Box R Ranch, Cora, Wyoming

It's also what made Jean Calmen Bratkovich buy her first horse when she was a forty-eight-year-old widow living in Detroit. Having toyed with the idea for a while, she finally did it when her new fiancé said to her, "At what age do you plan on getting this horse you've wanted your whole life?" Bratkovich moved to a small ranch in Idaho soon after, taking her gelding (and her fiancé) with her. That was in 1998.

After her second husband died, Bratkovich took her horse on another adventure through uncharted territory—a one-day cattle drive in the foothills of the Owyhee Mountains. She didn't know what to expect and was worried about how her flatlands horse would react to both the unfamiliar terrain and the cattle.

"It had taken me quite a while after my second husband's death by cancer to get back on my feet (or on horseback), both financially and emotionally," she says. "Getting up the courage for the cattle drive was a big thing."

When Bratkovich and her horse arrived, several hundred cows were already gathered. "They were coming toward us. You could feel the tension in him and in me. We were able to move to the side, and he got a look at what they were, and then we fell in behind."

Once she knew her horse would be fine, Bratkovich could relax and enjoy the ride. "It was a beautiful spring day, and I admired the view," she says. "We drove them some distance. It was pure joy being out in a different kind of place, knowing it was new and something I'd never done. Part of why this was important to me was that it led to my doing other things that were more difficult in the future, like camping out overnight in the mountains.

"Any time you accept a little challenge, it makes you better able to accept a bigger challenge. Every easy step is a preparation for a more difficult one."

BUILD YOUR OWN PIECE OF FURNITURE

If you were obsessed with Eleanor Roosevelt like I was in my teens, you'd know that in 1925, she and some friends started a tiny furniture company in Hyde Park, New York, called Val-Kill Industries. She did this to create work for local farmers in the winter, so they wouldn't have to leave the area to supplement their income. For Roosevelt, furniture building was a way to transform the lives of others.

For Wendy Feuer, it was a way to transform her own life.

Feuer, who's forty-eight, spent her childhood and adolescence building things. She built with Legos, Lincoln Logs, and model kits, and was immersed in projects for hours at a time. When she gave it up, Feuer lost an important aspect of her life: the joy of doing things with her hands. But she didn't know she missed it until she was nearly forty and took a woodworking workshop for women.

"I was feeling burned out," says Feuer. "I kept asking: *How do I fill myself back up?* I wondered what it was like to take a course outside of your comfort zone, what it was like to start from zero."

Her first project for class: build a box.

"I had never worked with tools, and it was a struggle," Feuer says. "Sawing, marking accurately, drilling to make the holes for the dowels so the sides fit together, and drawing lines with a fine-tip pencil to make it come out square—everything had to come out precise for the box to fit together. By the end of the weekend, I was physically tired but rejuvenated. Even though I was the slowest person in the class, there was something really powerful that I was getting back."

"Building furniture is so meditative. I can be stressed out about certain things, and then I go to my workshop—and instead of my mind being caught up in replaying all my worries, it gets caught up in the creativity. You see things transformed before your very eyes. That's very fulfilling to me."

(WOOD) SHOP TALK

- Chamfer: corner of a board beveled at a forty-five-degree angle
- Countersink: to set a screw head at or below the surface
- Crosscut: cut across the grain
- Dado: channel cut across the board, into which a second piece of wood is fitted
- Dowel: wooden pin used to provide strength and alignment
- Kerf: width of the blade
- Miter cut: angle cut across the width or thickness of the board
- Rabbet: L-shaped cut
- Rip cut: cut with the grain

Feuer has continued taking woodworking workshops over the years. In the summer of 2007, she made her largest piece, a Shaker breakfast table. In the fall of 2007, she made a small, round-top walnut table. But the piece she's most proud of is the blanket chest she started in the winter of 2008. She made all the joints by hand: twenty-four mortises and twenty-four tenons. "I'm still working on the lead," she says. "It's very painstaking.

"Every time I start a workshop and I see what we're supposed to make, my reaction is 'I'm not going to be able to do it.' But step by step, I go from someone who says, 'I can't do this' to 'Yes I can.' It's been empowering. I've developed greater confidence, and I believe in possibility."

ORGANIZE A RALLY

If Jane Vandenburgh had done what I typically do—become out-raged by something and then do nothing about it—750,000 women might never have marched on Washington on Mother's Day in 2000 to protest gun violence.

One year earlier, on April 20, 1999, two students from Columbine High School in Colorado shot and killed twelve classmates and a teacher. It was Vandenburgh's fifty-first birthday. At her celebration dinner that night, Vandenburgh couldn't stop talking about it. She'd had enough of gun violence. Earlier that year, a teenage couple from her daughter's high school had been shot dead in the street by a jilted ex-boyfriend.

"I thought there had to be a reaction . . . and a way to react," says Vandenburgh. "I had participated in demonstrations against the war in Vietnam. I understood the big show of strength on the street. It did ultimately make the people in Washington listen. We needed a ground-swell, a public sign."

Four months later, on August 10, a gunman shot at a group of chil-dren at a Los Angeles Jewish community center, spurring a New Jersey mother and public-relations executive named Donna Dees-Thomases to action. Within weeks, Dees-Thomases had launched a website for an organization called Million Mom March and had obtained a permit to hold a demonstration on the National Mall. On Labor Day, she publicly announced the march.

Vandenburgh called the number on the website and signed on to get things moving in Washington; Dees-Thomases joined her there for an initial meeting of volunteers. There were nine people in the room, five of them children. "It had that very shaky feeling that we'd have a meeting and nobody would come," says Vandenburgh. "There was a core of people in the metro area, and we tried to meet every week to plan these actions. We were trying to find people who could help us."

Among the first were congresswomen Carolyn McCarthy, Connie Morella, and Sheila Jackson-Lee. Weeks after the march was announced, they stood on the steps of the Capitol to voice their support. That was also the day the Million Mom March T-shirts arrived. Vandenburgh's daughter Eva, who was fourteen, grabbed a toddler-size shirt and put it on for the press conference. Eva appeared on the news in her tight cropped tee and appealed to the youth of America. "Come to the march," she said, "and we'll put you up."

"The day we stood there, that was when there was a Million Mom March," says Vandenburgh. "We had T-shirts; we had a website; we had business cards and invented our own titles." (Hers was metro coordinator.) "It was absolutely seat-of-the-pants."

After that, things started taking off. Women from around the country volunteered to be coordinators. Grassroots activists got involved. Other groups donated office space and phone lines. Celebrities started lining up. And the media started paying attention.

"Instead of us calling them, they called us every time there was a shooting," says Vandenburgh. "Then the heroes started to show up. These were the women who had lost children. The stories of these people are just breathtaking. If this cause became our church, these were our saints."

On the day of the march, an estimated 750,000 people gathered on the Mall to hear speeches by Rosie O'Donnell, Susan Sarandon, Hillary Rodham Clinton, and mothers and grandmothers who'd lost children to gun violence. "Until eight weeks beforehand, we didn't have a phone number," says Vandenburgh. "It could have so easily not happened."

GET HYPNOTIZED

Make fun of it if you want, but women who've been hypnotized know the truth: A trance can be better than good sex and a long nap combined. Undergoing hypnosis is one of the most deeply relaxing, stress-relieving things you can do—and yes, it really can help you get over your nail-biting habit, fear of flying, writer's block, and so on.

Worried that you'll wind up barking like a dog or pulling down your pants in public? If you do make a spectacle of yourself, it won't be because you've been hypnotized. Even in a trance, you're awake enough to reject any suggestion that you don't want to follow. "You're aware of things going on, of sounds and sensations," explains Nancy, who's forty-seven. "But another part of you is completely divorced from those sensations and from any anxiety you have in your life. If my nose itches, I'll say to myself that my nose itches, but I don't feel like I need to scratch it."

Nancy sought hypnosis because she was so stressed out about a public-speaking engagement that she couldn't sleep. Something was wrong with the speech she'd written, but she couldn't figure out what it was. Her first session began with deep-breathing exercises. Then the hypnotherapist put a quarter in her upturned palm and told her that when her hand moved on its own and dropped the quarter, she would be in a trance. She had Nancy close her eyes and picture herself walking down a road, passing numbered signposts as she went. As the therapist guided her through this walk, Nancy relaxed, and at the tenth signpost, her hand started jerking around and the quarter fell.

The therapist made the positive posthypnosis suggestions they had discussed ahead of time: "I will not be nervous. It will be fun. I'll figure out what's wrong with my speech." When she came out of the trance, Nancy wasn't sure that the hypnosis had done anything for her. But as she walked along the street on her way home, it came to her: The beginning of her speech was all wrong, and she'd have to rewrite it. That night she slept. When she got to her engagement, she wasn't nervous at all. "I realized I knew my speech," she says. "I was so happy to be there. That one time cured me of all my fears of public speaking."

A TRANCE FOR ALL WOMEN

There are many methods for inducing trances. Abby Cooperberg, a certified hypnotist, uses this one on herself:

- Sit in bed or in a comfortable chair and do some deep breathing to relax.
- To get into a trance, say to yourself: "I see three things . . ." and name them; followed by "I feel three things . . ." and "I hear three things. . . ."
- Repeat the process, naming two items, and then just one.
- Then go in reverse, starting with one item and going back up to three.

The first method you try might not succeed. But don't give up. Try a different technique . . . or a different therapist. One is bound to work for you.

LEARN TRAPEZE

Travel back in time to the playgrounds of your youth and imagine being on a swing. You pump your legs like crazy to get some momentum going, then lean all the way back, feet pointing at the sun, rising higher and higher. Your hair flaps behind you; your stomach flutters. Soon you're swinging so high that the chain has slackened, and you wonder for a second if you're going to go right over the top of the swing set.

Swinging is great.

To recapture the joy of swooping and soaring, you can head to the nearest schoolyard and try cramming your butt into a swing. Or you can do it adult-style and take trapeze lessons. They're easier to find than you may think. In recent years, trapeze schools have popped up everywhere from Baltimore to Gilbert, Arizona, to inside the Jordan's Furniture store in Reading, Massachusetts. They're not expensive, either. You can connect with your inner Wallenda for as little as $45 for a two-hour introductory class.

Jody Ordioni had wanted to try trapeze ever since she saw Carrie Bradshaw take lessons on *Sex and the City*. For her forty-ninth birthday, a friend gave her a gift certificate for a group lesson at the Trapeze School of New York, on the Hudson River. "I was so excited," says Ordioni. "I would have never done it on my own. I'm always so busy; it just would have gone on that list of things you always want to do."

The weather on the first day of class was perfect—sunny, warm, and breezy. After some brief instruction on the ground, Ordioni and her classmates put on girdle-tight harnesses and climbed, one by one, up the ladder to the trapeze—about three stories up. "I was terrified after ten steps," she says. "When you get to the top, you have to walk out onto this small plank. Imagine when you climb onto a ladder and you're on the top rung: You have to put your feet up where your hands are, but there's nothing to put your hands on."

Nothing except the hunk of an instructor who's waiting to hook ropes onto your harness and say encouraging things, which this is a good time for. Once you're hooked up, you hold on to the ropes and walk to the end of the plank, then stand there with your feet hanging halfway off. The instructor gives you the trapeze bar, and one of your hands has to leave the ropes to grab it. When your other hand follows, you're off the plank and flying.

Trick number one: Swing and bring your knees to your chest. Trick number two: Pull your feet up and over the trapeze bar. Trick number three: Remove your hands and swing upside down by your legs. Ordioni did this routine five or six times. By the end, she couldn't get up that ladder quick enough. "All the fear disappears," she says. "You don't even realize you're going up."

For her final feat, Ordioni had to swing upside down and connect in midair with an instructor, who was also swinging upside down on the other side. On her third swing, the instructor grabbed Ordioni by the wrists, and she had to free her legs from the bar and swing with him holding her arms. "At that point, I could have done anything," she says. "If they'd said, 'Do three back flips,' I would have said, 'Sure!'"

GO COMMANDO

done

I t's been nearly two decades since Sharon Stone got flashy with Michael Douglas in *Basic Instinct,* and we're still gossiping over the spectacle of women without panties. It was scandalous then, and it's even more so now, after Lindsay Lohan's and Britney Spears's tabloid spreads. But for women who regularly go bottomless, such public displays totally defeat the purpose, which is to take it all off without anyone knowing it.

Everyone loves a secret, and walking around the mall with nothing on under your pants is a good one. If it makes you feel sexy, that's nobody's business but your own. In fact, for most commandos the idea of being found out—let alone seen—is mortifying. Maybe this isn't the kind of secret you want to keep. That's understandable. There are a million reasons not to shed your panties, chief among them:

- It's drafty.
- It feels weird.
- It's naughty.

To which aficionados would respond:

- Naughty can be nice.
- It's not as weird as having a thong crawl up your butt or elastic leg bands around your thighs.
- When the wind blows and you're wearing a skirt, you catch a nice breeze.

Women who go commando say it's more comfortable. And really, who needs underpants, anyway?

You may. But even if the whole thing turns you off, you've got to have some questions about life without panties. Kriss Kovach, a forty-two-year-old commando veteran, explains it.

THE LIST: What's the real kick in going commando?
KRISS KOVACH: It feels like, *Oh my god, I'm getting away with this and nobody knows.*

TL: When is it most fun for you?
KK: I lecture at a large university, so sometimes when I'm lecturing, I think about it and smile. You know how they say, "If you're nervous about speaking, just picture everyone in the audience without their clothes on"? For me, it's the opposite. I think, *Ha ha, I'm not wearing any underwear.* It bolsters my confidence.

TL: Okay, but how does it *feel?*
KK: It's sensual. There's less of a barrier—literally and figuratively. If you see someone you find physically attractive and you're aware of it, well . . . let's say the "zing factor" is less muted.

TL: Is it cold under there?
KK: I think it's warmer. Like how if you're in bed naked, under a comforter, it's warmer than if you're in silk pajamas under the comforter. It's body heat.

TL: Do you ever wear underpants?
KK: If I'm wearing a short skirt, I'll put on a pair of silk tap pants. I'm not going to show the business; I'm not into that. And when I go to the doctor, I wear a pair of plain-Jane underpants.

TL: What happens when you get your period?
KK: I have really light periods—only three days. Plus, I use one of those cups that catches the blood, the Moon Cup, so the period is not an issue. If you have heavy periods or have to wear a pad, then you'd need underwear. And maybe a tampon string is uncomfortable.

TL: Not to be gross, but what about secretions?
KK: For me, it's like the periods—I just don't have a lot of that. So I don't know.

VISIT AN ASHRAM

Whether we realize it or not, most of us are searching for peace, clarity, and calmness in our lives. These are good things—far better than conflict, self-doubt, and inner turmoil. But few of us would pick up and travel eight thousand miles, or even one hundred miles, to find them at an ashram. Perhaps we should. Many women who've sought enlightenment through meditation say it's changed their lives.

In her best-selling memoir *Eat, Pray, Love,* Elizabeth Gilbert writes about her yearlong quest for wholeness following a painful divorce, a failed romance, and a bout of depression. In that year, she spent four months in Italy indulging in life's pleasures, four months in India seeking devotion, and four months in Indonesia looking for balance. But her journey started at an ashram in upstate New York—the same rustic, funky place where Sherry Davis first started down the spiritual path of Siddha Yoga.

Davis, who's fifty-five, wasn't looking for anything in particular when she and her husband first went to Shree Muktananda Ashram in South Fallsburg, New York, but she was definitely looking for something. "I knew there were deeper places in me," she says.

She found them at the ashram. The goal of Siddha Yoga is to awaken the kundalini, the divine energy that supposedly lies dormant in a coil at the base of the spine. Once it's released, this energy travels up the spinal column and begins to purify the entire being. When it reaches the crown of the head, the soul merges into the supreme Self and attains a state of Self-realization. During the meditation process at the ashram, Swami Muktananda, or Baba, as he was known, went from devotee to devotee, physically opening the channels in their spine to release the force.

"When Baba walked behind me, he gave me a kick in the bottom of my spine," says Davis. "At the same time, he took his fingers and twisted my nose. I opened my eyes and I saw thousands of raindrop crystals that looked like rainbows. I felt this surge of energy through my circuitry. I felt like I was floating. From that moment on I was a different person ... more one with everybody."

SIDDHA YOGA BASICS

- Honor your Self, Worship your Self, Meditate on your Self; God dwells within you, as you.
- See God in each other.
- The heart is the hub of all sacred places; go there and roam.
- Nothing exists that is not Shiva (a Hindu deity).

Davis and her husband continued visiting the ashram for meditation intensives over the weekends or during the summer; they sometimes took their children along. In 1995, Davis fractured her ankle right before going to a three-day silent meditation intensive, which meant she'd have to sit with her foot elevated instead of doing the yoga poses. She went to the ashram anyway, and before the intensive began, she sat in the round temple in front of a beautiful statue of the guru known as Bade Baba.

"I kept looking at this statue of him and thought, *I want to participate fully in the meditation. I know people ask you for things all the time, but can you heal me?*"

When Davis stood up, her ankle no longer hurt. And she had no doubt whatsoever.

SHOOT A GUN

I could no sooner see myself shooting a gun than harpooning a whale or lassoing a steer. I didn't grow up around guns (or whales or steer), although I did take riflery one year at summer camp. I've never held a gun or even seen one up close—which is why the idea of firing one is so fascinating, I'm sure. It's like those dreams in which you land a solid punch or outrun a bad guy—feats so unlikely in your waking hours that you've got to act them out in your sleep.

For the uninitiated like me, the question is, why would you even want to shoot a gun? Some women do it for fun, I guess. I'm not sure I'd set up a row of cans on my back deck, but I could see going to a skeet-shooting range on the weekends. (I once read a piece in *Esquire* about Rosario Dawson shooting skeet. She made it sound fun.) But many women must take it up with a purpose in mind.

Jan Donaldson learned to shoot when she was fifty-eight, for very practical reasons: She was divorced and living alone in a town that had seen a spate of attacks on women. In one assault, a woman her age had come out of the supermarket (the same one Donaldson goes to) in the middle of the day, pushed her shopping cart to her car (right where Donaldson usually parks), and been held up by two boys with guns.

"I thought, *Okay, I'm by myself, and I'm not having this. I'm not going to be afraid,*" says Donaldson. "I never thought I'd be in that place, but there was no question that I would shoot a gun to save my own life. I decided I would never be someone's victim."

She bought a Smith & Wesson at a local gun store, and got both a regular gun permit and a concealed-carry license so she could keep the revolver in her car. She took lessons from the shop owner at his shooting range—complete with those moving paper targets that rush up to assault you. "The sensation I had when I was hitting the target was relief. It wasn't too hard, I wasn't too weak, and I wasn't too fearful. It made me feel more in charge of my life."

Jane Corwin didn't learn to shoot for her own protection, or for pure fun. She learned for the sake of her dog—an English setter with a gift for hunting. Corwin, who's forty-six, had entered him in a hunt test, a performance competition that the American Kennel Club holds for the pointing breeds, and he was a natural. But he needed more hunting time, his trainer said, which meant Corwin was going to have to take him.

Corwin took a state hunter-education program and got a license, then signed up for an Introduction to Shooting Sports class. After borrowing her father's shotgun (she later bought her own "ladies' revolver"), she spent the whole day at the trap range. "I wasn't nervous about the gun," she says. "I was nervous about being good at it. I pulled the trigger plenty of times without hitting the target. I'm still not a good shot, but I do my best."

taped myself singing

RECORD YOUR OWN MUSIC

When you used to sing into your hairbrush every morning—or into the wind as you drove your Malibu convertible down the highway—who were you? Nancy Sinatra? Toni Tennille? Tina Turner? It doesn't matter. The point is, you had the music in you. You were as good as any of those girls, only nobody knew it. You deserved to have your own record....

If you still have the music in you, you can make a CD fairly easily now. All it takes is time, money, and an audio engineer with a studio you can rent. With the proliferation of affordable home recording equipment and portable vocal booths, it may be harder to find an available engineer than it is to find the time and funds to hire him.

When you record a CD, you're making a pledge to yourself. You're basically saying, *I have talent, passion, and vision, and I'm going to pursue them come hell or high water.* And the longer you wait to put your TPV on a disc, the sweeter it is when you do. Just ask Elaine Brown.

In 1997, Brown of Calgary, Canada, began taking voice lessons with her daughter. In 2004, after performing in choirs and choruses for years, she recorded a CD entitled *Elaine—Look at Me* (available at www.elainejeanbrown.com). She was fifty-six. For more of her story, see "Take Singing Lessons" on page 124.

My friend's cousin Amy Hobish, a singer-songwriter for more than twenty years, doesn't know yet where her CD will take her. After three years of painstaking work, she's almost finished making it. In some ways, that recording has been in the works since the mid-'80s, when Hobish became sick with mercury poisoning and had to put her musical aspirations on hold while she sought accurate diagnosis and treatment.

"All the way through, I would continue to write songs, but I couldn't have a career. I had no continuity," Hobish says. "I've been granted a reprieve, and I'm doing it—all on my own terms. I've written it, played it, sung it, arranged it, produced it, and financed it." Hobish moved to Los Angeles to make the CD, after selling her New York apartment to pay for it. She found an engineer she liked (and could afford), and has been going to the studio for anywhere from twenty to sixty hours a week. Even when she's not recording, she's still focused on the CD.

Still, Hobish says, doing it feels right.

"When someone says they'd like to play on my record, that's exciting. The music is the thrill—the actual music. It's taken forever, but I needed to have something on this planet that was an expression of the deepest part of me."

DAVE MATTHEWS, BOB DYLAN, AND YOU

If you're ever in Memphis and have money to spend, you can record your music where the likes of Led Zeppelin, Tanya Tucker, and the White Stripes recorded theirs. For around $1,200 a day, Ardent Studios will provide you with an engineer and an assistant, and for an extra fee, it will arrange for any backup you need, from a bass player to a horn section. There are plenty of other major studios that rent time to aspiring Beyoncés, so don't hesitate to inquire.

Done

BUY YOURSELF
A SEX TOY

When it comes to buying a sex toy, there's no sense in being bashful. It's perfectly natural to wonder about erotic gadgets: What do they look like? Where do they go? How do they *feel?* And, most important, who do you know who uses them? Considering how many vibrators, dildos, and other pleasure products are tucked away in women's underwear drawers across the country, the answer may well be everyone.

Playing with sex toys might seem risqué to you, but there's nothing new or radical about it. The world's oldest known dildo, in fact, dates back to the Upper Paleolithic period. Today, the $1.5 billion "adult novelties" industry is booming, thanks to the Internet and the anonymity it provides. No more worries about being spotted at the local sex shop—now you can buy from the privacy of your own home. You can linger over the products, laugh over names like Sally Sea Twist and Shake, and order with the perverse pleasure of knowing that the UPS guy will be carrying a pulsating purple phallus to your door without realizing it.

Some women are dragged into sex shops by hopeful husbands or by friends who've already seen the light. Others go willingly, in search of anything that might fire up a dormant or dull sex life. (Sound familiar?) Still others are there to please themselves when there's no partner in sight. No matter what their motivation, most women who check out the merchandise become very satisfied customers. And why wouldn't they? Vibrators are designed to hit pleasure spots you probably never knew existed.

Happily, there is a sex toy—and a sex-toy website—for everyone. If you're squeamish about the whole thing, check out Babeland.com. This site is warm, bright, and very girlie. Even the product names are cute: Snugglepuss, Rabbit Habit, and the Bunny Love Kit. The site also provides nonthreatening advice on everything from how to choose a lube to how to find your G-spot.

If you're more comfortable with a clinical approach, try Talksexwithsue.com. Sue Johanson is a no-nonsense sex therapist from Canada who has a weekly show on Oxygen. Sue tells it like it is, providing in-depth information on every sexual topic imaginable. She also reviews products and sells them through her website.

But the best product endorsements come from women whose sex lives have been transformed by their toys. For ten years, my friend Liz's medication made having an orgasm impossible for her, yet she wouldn't even consider trying sex aids. "My husband always felt so bad, but I resisted getting a vibrator," says Liz, who's forty-seven. "Maybe it's because I'm a Catholic; it's a good-girl thing. I finally said okay . . . and it was great!"

Orgasms weren't all the vibrator added to her sex life. After fourteen years of marriage, says Liz, "We knew everything about our bodies. This is a new way of being intimate. There's a deep feeling of being together. It makes me feel young."

What more do you need to know?

TAKE A LOVER

If you want something in life, you've got to reach out and take it. That's the kind of thing my grandfather used to tell me, probably because I'm a girl and he didn't think I'd figure it out on my own. He was right, though. Being passive gets you nowhere fast, which is why people don't walk around saying, "If you want something in life, you've got to reach out and wait for somebody to drop it in your lap."

Maybe what you want right now is a sexual liaison—a new man or woman to spice up your life. That's great, but don't just "have" an affair, like you have an accident. If you want a lover, *take* a lover. Be grabby about it. Claim it for yourself. If you're stepping out on a spouse or a partner, only you will know whether it's worth the risk. Whether you're committed or single, as long as you're going there, go with gusto.

There's nothing casual about taking a lover. Ask Lady Chatterley. Lovers don't just sleep with you; they fill a void. There are lovers to hold and caress you; lovers to excite you; lovers to listen to you, shower you with gifts, or help you escape. Lovers can help you explore new horizons—lesbian sex, fantasy sex, whatever. If all you want is revenge or a thrill, go to a bar and pick someone up. Between lovers, there are always more, no matter how long the relationship lasts.

> **"I was so starved for attention, it was like a slice of nirvana. I mourned [my lover] more than my divorce. But I have no regrets."**
>
> —Leslie, age 48

My friend Leslie took a lover after her divorce, and while she slept with him only twice, she describes it as "the hugest affair of my life." What started as an email exchange with a man she knew from college became an intense relationship with daily messages full of sexy talk.

"I was so starved for attention, it was like a slice of nirvana," says Leslie, who's forty-eight. "I mourned him more than my divorce. But I have no regrets." Borrowing a term from author Gail Sheehy, she adds: "He was my pilot-light lover."

What can a lover ignite in you? Perhaps simply a desire for sex. I know a woman who began an affair for the feeling of power it gave her, and she continued it because her lover gave her orgasms for the first time in her life. He made her feel like a sexual being in a way her husband or previous lovers couldn't. Thanks to him, she craved sex for the pleasure it gave her, not someone else. Imagine if she had never met him. Imagine if you took a lover who did the same thing for you.

Maybe a lover can rekindle your passion—not just for sex, but also for many other pursuits in life. It's like giving your battery a boost; once your energy is renewed, it flows in all directions. You might find yourself returning to yoga class, taking drawing lessons, or asking for a promotion. Who knows—you might even pour more effort and energy into your marriage, and find new passion there.

When you take a lover, as opposed to having an affair, you're taking something important for yourself. And that's no accident.

HIKE
MACHU PICCHU

There's a difference between a vacation and a trip; a trip and a trek; and a trek and a journey. A vacation takes you to Cinderella's Castle at Disney World; a trip takes you to the Sistine Chapel in Rome; a trek takes you to the bottom of the Grand Canyon; and a journey takes you roughly 11,000 feet above sea level to a lodge on the Inca Trail facing the twin Andean pinnacles of Salkantay and Umantay.

"You're looking at these gorgeous, glacier-laden peaks, and the clouds are going by and you're in church," says Liz Becker, who made her first journey along the trail to Machu Picchu in October 2007, when she was forty-two.

People often use spiritual terms when they talk about Machu Picchu, the ancient Incan city built on a mountain ridge in Peru, nearly eight thousand feet above sea level. If you wonder why, go online and look at pictures—they'll give you an idea. But you'll never fully understand until you actually walk through the City in the Clouds.

Kathleen Curran, who's fifty-eight, went to Peru for three weeks when she was between jobs. She'd always wanted to go; in college, she had loved studying the Inca. After spending two weeks in the Amazon, she flew to Cusco, the capital of the Inca empire and the starting point for Machu Picchu excursions. Cusco is eleven thousand feet above sea level, and many tourists spend a few days there getting acclimatized. Or not.

Curran experienced a setback on day one. After having roast pork and cold beer for lunch, she started to hike up to Sacsayhuamán, an ancient walled complex built from limestone. (Incan construction is a mystery—the stones, some weighing tons, are laid so close together, you can't even slip a razor between them.) As she climbed, Curran detected a pinprick in her neck that soon felt like an ice pick in the base of her skull. She spent the next two days in bed suffering from altitude sickness.

When she recovered, Curran zigzagged through the Andes mountains on a three-hour train ride to the town of Aguas Caliente, where she caught a bus to Machu Picchu (you can also walk there from the city; it takes about ninety minutes). She hiked a trail up to Huayna Picchu, a summit overlooking the ruins. "You can see the layout of Machu Picchu," she says. "You look down on the clouds, down on the river. You really feel that it's a spiritual place."

Liz Becker felt that way when she looked out at the peak of Salkantay, which is known as the Savage Mountain. "For centuries, the Andean people have looked at this mountain in awe," she says, "and you can feel it in the earth."

Becker went to Machu Picchu on a six-day hiking tour along the Salkantay Trail, a hidden route that was developed as an alternative to the traditional Inca Trail. After walking three to six hours a day, each night the group ended up at a different lodge, where they could relax in a hot tub, drink cocktails, and sleep in comfortable beds with nice sheets.

Becker loved the entire experience—the history, beauty, culture, and cocktails—so much that she's planning to lead her own group tour for professional women. She's calling it "The Machu Picchu Adventure: A Women's Leadership Journey."

done

HAVE NUDE
PICTURES TAKEN

Why do it? Why traipse around in the buff, vamping it up for the camera? *Oh, it's not like that. If I did it, it would be more like art.* Okay—then why loll around in the nude, posing artistically for the camera?

Here's why:

- It's fun.
- It's flirty.
- It's daring.
- It's sexy.
- It's a testament to how you feel about your body, and how little you care about what other people think.

If you're toying with the idea of posing nude—whether you're draped over a chaise or straddling a kitchen chair—you've chosen the right time. Nude is in. Or, more accurately, it's out . . . on display. Think of all the skin you've seen lately: Lindsay Lohan as Marilyn Monroe in *New York* magazine; Scarlett Johansson and Keira Knightley on the cover of *Vanity Fair;* and, in the spirit of Demi Moore, Christina Aguilera and her pregnant belly on the cover of *Marie Claire*.

Two naked actresses that you probably didn't see were Hilary Swank and Penélope Cruz in the 2007 Pirelli calendar. Filled with glamorous, and often nude, photos of women, the calendar is available only to a select group of about thirty thousand VIPs. But you can check out the photos at Pirelli.com.

Yes, the women mentioned above are all under forty. But the Pirelli calendar also featured a very sexy seventy-one-year-old Sophia Loren lying on a bed, tangled in sheets, wearing a see-through black dress. "I enjoyed myself, posing as if I was a little girl again," she said in an interview. And Jamie Lee Curtis, who's fifty, recently went topless for a cover shoot in *AARP* magazine. The photo shows her standing in a swimming pool in water up to her chest. "I feel way better now than I did when I was twenty," she says.

Even regular women feel good enough about themselves to show off their bodies. Kate, who's forty-one, recently took nude pictures of herself to send to an old boyfriend/artist to paint from. In the process, she made a shocking discovery: She likes looking at herself. Despite the fact that she'd had three children, the photos were beautiful. (The ex-boyfriend's new girlfriend wasn't so crazy about them, and neither was Kate's husband, but that's a much longer story.)

"I think this is the time of life to do these things," Kate says. "When I was young, I always did edgy things, but I never did nudity. I wasn't comfortable in my own skin."

Neither was Spike, who's forty-four. Not long ago, however, she was organizing a nude calendar as a local fundraiser. On a whim, she called the photographer on the project and asked if she would take some nude shots of Spike. Spike had lost forty pounds after her divorce and had a great new boyfriend, so why not? "My biggest fear was that she was either going to hit on me or laugh at me," she says. "I have stretch marks, and gravity has taken a toll on my breasts."

The photographer neither laughed at nor made a pass at her, and Spike is very glad she had those pictures taken. "I grew up in a very modest Catholic family; I never saw anyone naked," she says. "I wish I hadn't grown up with all this false modesty. Taking the pictures was freeing, in a fun way. It was nuttiness."

HAVE A COSMETIC SURGERY PROCEDURE

Your feminist foremothers would die if they knew you were considering cosmetic surgery. How could you? It's demeaning and objectifying, and besides, you're beautiful just the way you are. Wrinkles, sags, and bags are nothing to be ashamed of. You should celebrate your maturing body, not bow to cultural stereotypes.

No more waxing your chin or coloring your hair. Take off your Wonderbra and burn it. Toss all your makeup and moisturizers. You don't need that stuff.

Maybe not, but what if you want it? What if you don't feel like celebrating what's happened to your body? Are you supposed to love your frown lines and low-swinging breasts, or simply tolerate them for another thirty years? We hear all the time that we live in a youth-obsessed culture, as if it's a bad thing. Would it be better to obsess over joint pain and bone loss? The truth is, people are staying younger longer. We have babies in our forties, we work into our seventies, and we live into our nineties. We certainly don't act like we're old—so why should we look like it if we don't want to?

This isn't an endorsement of cosmetic surgery (not that any liberated woman needs one, anyway). Personally speaking, I would rather have bags down to my ankles than get any procedure involving needles, scalpels, and complication risks. But I'll do whatever else I can to fight the ravages of time (see "Get a Makeover," page 130). And I certainly understand if you want to lift it up, pull it back, or cut it out.

My friend Leslie, who's forty-eight, never imagined she'd get a boob job. But after nursing two kids she hated what had become of her breasts—they were smaller and lower, with big nipples—and she wanted her body back. Her mother had been begging her to get the surgery and offering to pay, so after Leslie got divorced, she took her up on it.

"I had lost so much volume after my nursing," she says. "Because I had boobs when I was younger, it made me much more relaxed about wanting them. It would have felt more vain, somehow, if I hadn't."

Still, it took Leslie a year to get used to her new breasts. "At first, I was shocked and appalled by how big they seemed. I didn't want to feel like I was a bimbo," she says. "I didn't like them until I started dating—until I bought a special dress and a pretty bra. I knew I felt sexy, and that I hadn't felt that way before.

"There are times when I'm getting dressed that I say, 'Yes!' If I want to, I can have cleavage. I could in high school and in college, and I can now. I always wore a camisole in my marriage. It's nice to wear a nice bra. There's a power in feeling attractive."

More power to you.

DRIVE OVER 100 MILES PER HOUR

When you were a young woman, being called "fast" was no compliment. It meant you were a floozy, a hussy, maybe even a slut. Thankfully, nobody thinks like that anymore. You can do all kinds of things—strip, kiss a stranger, sleep with a younger man—without raising too many eyebrows. (For details, see pages 22, 136, and 210.)

To see just how far we've come, visit Fastwomen4u.com, where you'll find tiny figurines of hot babes in bikinis and short shorts washing miniscule model cars—all made of durable cold-cast resin. They have itty-bitty stacked heels and great hairdos, and if you don't have a problem with their being demeaning, you might buy a few for your dresser top. They're adorable.

These girls are fast in more ways than one, which is part of their appeal. They not only wash cars; they also actually race them. They've got sex appeal plus guts, spunk, and a penchant for speed. Check out the lyrics to their theme song:

Fast Women! Coming at you at the speed of sound.
Fast Women! Leaving tread marks burning in the ground.
Fast Women! Popping clutches to be glory bound.
Fast Women! Fast Women!

If being a fast woman means you get to whip around a racetrack at 150 miles per hour, I say bring it on. And if you want to do it in heels, more power to you. Who cares what you wear? You finally have a chance to release the speed demon in you without getting pulled over and arrested.

If you're like Linda Engelhardt, you've been pushing that envelope for years. Engelhardt loves going fast. Many times she's driven 85 miles an hour, and once she even hit 100. "I'm more comfortable driving fast," she says. "I feel like I have to be alert when I drive slower, because there are drivers I have to watch out for."

WHERE TO BURN RUBBER

- Memphis Motorsports Park, Memphis, Tennessee
- Pocono Raceway, Long Pond, Pennsylvania
- Jeff Gordon and Mario Andretti Racing School, fifteen speedways across America
- Richard Petty Driving Experience, twenty-five speedways across America

Four years ago, for her fiftieth birthday, Engelhardt's husband gave her a $500 gift certificate for a NASCAR driving experience at the Pocono Raceway in Pennsylvania. There were ten people in her class; nine were middle-aged men. After a brief talk about how to drive at high speeds, the instructor loaded them into a van for a couple of laps around the track. Engelhardt paid extra to have the instructor take her around a few more times in a car before she went out on her own.

"It was the most frightening experience I've ever had," she says. "As the passenger, it's frightening because they go 160 miles per hour. My stomach was jumping from side to side. I started doubting myself: *Do I really have the guts to do this?* When I got out of the car and remembered I was the only woman in the group, I said, 'How could I not do this?'"

Engelhardt put on a jumpsuit and a helmet, got in her racecar, and did eight laps around the track in eight minutes. "My hands gripped the steering wheel so tightly," she says. "I couldn't relax until my fifth lap, and then it was like, *Oh, I'm liking this.*"

done

LEARN AN EXOTIC DANCE

Latin dances generate heat—that's what makes them so sexy. The merengue, rumba, samba, and others make your body desperate to move. In addition, they are deeply rooted in the cultures they come from—merengue is from the Dominican Republic; rumba is from Cuba; samba is from Brazil—so learning them is like a mini–foreign exchange program. When you're out on the floor, you not only dance Brazilian, you also *feel* a little Brazilian.

As spicy as those dances are, however, they aren't nearly as passion filled or transportive as flamenco (think castanets, ruffled skirts, and *clickety-clack* shoes). The five-hundred-year-old gypsy dance comes from the same region in southern Spain where bullfighting started, so you can imagine what a fiery culture *that* is. The U.S. has a tight community of aficionados promoting the flamenco spirit and lifestyle, and depending on how involved you get, flamenco can be a lifelong passion.

For Julie Tilsner, one of flamenco's main draws was that it's a dance that favors maturity over youth. The greater your life experience, the more emotion and depth you can bring to the dance, and the better a flamenco dancer you'll be.

Tilsner, who is forty-three, was a belly dancer in college and for a few years afterward. She'd always wanted to learn flamenco, but she didn't pursue it until she was middle-aged with two children, in a crumbling marriage, and desperate to do something good for herself. The tipping point came when her stepmother died six weeks after being diagnosed with cancer. Tilsner decided she didn't want to put flamenco off anymore and signed up for her first class.

She was hooked instantly. "If I had taken it when I was twenty, I would have gone to Spain," she says. "That's what you do. You study with the gypsies. You immerse yourself. I couldn't do that."

SPEAKING FLAMENCO

Baile: the dance
Duende: the soul force that inspires flamenco art
Gitano: gypsy
Jaleo: utterances of approval and encouragement; recognition of the *duende*
Juerga: flamenco party or jam session
Mantón: embroidered silk shawl with long fringe
Pitos: finger snaps that accompany flamenco song and dance
Quejío: lament
Toque: guitar playing

So Tilsner immersed herself in flamenco in the U.S. She took classes with different teachers and in different styles of the dance. She went to performances and attended workshops. She even started dating a renowned flamenco guitarist after she separated from her husband.

"You open a door a little way and you peek in, and you see something interesting and you walk in," Tilsner says. "Flamenco's beautiful and powerful and strong. There's so much about it I don't know. I'll never master it, but I don't mind that."

¡Olé!

Done

SWIM WITH SEA CREATURES

Perhaps your infatuation with sea creatures came from watching *Flipper* every Saturday night in the mid-'6os, or in reruns after that. The lovable, superintelligent dolphin was the "pet" of two brothers, Sandy and Bud, who lived in a marine preserve with their widowed (of course) park-ranger father. Each week, Flipper helped the boys through a crisis. He understood what they said and came when they called him. He talked adorable dolphin-talk and gave kisses. For kicks, Flipper would do a backward tail ride, and at the end of each show, when everyone was laughing, he'd cackle right along.

What's not to love? Gentle giants like dolphins and manatees are more like wet, blubbery dogs than prehistoric behemoths. They're caring, smart, and very soulful, and when humans have a chance to interact with them, they often feel a special connection. M. J. Miller was touched in a very meaningful way by her date with a manatee; she'll tell you it was the best thing she ever did.

Miller was approaching her fiftieth birthday and had just recovered from breast cancer the year before, so she wanted to do something fun to mark the occasion. She'd seen a video of a manatee swim, and that was it. The following winter, she and two girlfriends went to Florida to try it out for themselves.

They flew into Tampa and drove north for an hour to Clear River—manatee central. At seven the next morning, they were in their wetsuits on a guided boat tour, navigating the bays, tributaries, and lagoons where manatees swim during the winter. (The cold water drives them closer to the shore.) When the women found a good spot, they put on snorkeling gear and jumped in. They didn't have to look for the manatees; the manatees came straight to them.

"They swim all around you," says Miller, who is now fifty-five. "One came up underneath me and scared the life out of me. But it just wanted to be touched. It was really wonderful.

"They have a very rough hide, and when you're up close you can see these terrible scars from boats and propellers. You're only allowed to touch them with one hand, because they feel trapped if you use both.

"The babies will just lie by their mothers. The water is so clear, I could see them lying on the bottom. They're very quiet, very gentle. They don't like a lot of noise. There is something very calming about them."

Watching the manatees nurture their babies was soothing and spiritual for Miller. Her mother had died a year and half earlier, and suddenly Miller had a sense of her mother being there with her.

"I just kept thinking about my mother," Miller says. "She hated the water; she was not a swimmer. But with the manatees, there was this kind of attachment between the animal and the people. You saw these mothers taking care of their babies, and yet they wanted the human touch. They wanted the comfort."

So did Miller, it turns out, and she found it in a place she never expected to.

WHERE TO FROLIC WITH DOLPHINS

- Florida Keys
- Yucatán Peninsula, Mexico
- Hawaii
- The Bahamas
- New Zealand
- Azores archipelago
- Egypt (Red Sea)

37 *Done*

DIVE OFF A CLIFF

There are moments in life when you find yourself at the edge of the proverbial cliff, wondering if you're going to go for it or retreat to safety. And then there's a moment, if you put yourself there, when you find yourself on an actual cliff, wondering if you've completely lost your mind.

For Jan St. John, cliff diving in Costa Rica was both a figurative and a literal leap into uncharted waters. As you'll learn in "Skydive" (page 116), St. John, who's fifty-six, is on a campaign to break free from old habits and fears. An empty-nester with two grown daughters, she's made a conscious decision to live a fuller, larger life from now on. And that means taking risks and doing things she would never have done before—such as ziplining, white-water rafting, and cliff diving while on an eco-adventure with her oldest daughter.

"If I'm going to become an elder—which I will, God willing—I want to have something to offer," she says.

St. John and her daughter, who is twenty-seven, are both afraid of water—the result of having witnessed a drowning at the beach years ago. And yet they climbed to the top of a steep mountain, walking along a two-foot-wide path above a rushing river.

"This was not a calm pool of water," St. John says. "You had to dive in and let the river carry you for a mile. As I was going up, I couldn't even look down. It probably was the scariest thing I've ever done.

"You just stand there, at the edge of the cliff, and you have a choice. You can turn back. I had time to think: *Am I going to back away?*

If I do, I won't be redefining myself. So do I or don't I? Then my daughter said, 'Come on, Mom, you can do this.' I didn't want to show her I was a coward.

"The dive itself wasn't great—it was sheer terror! I kept thinking, *How deep will I go? Will I hit the bottom? Will they have to come in and get me?* You go way, way, way, way down. But then you come to the top, and it's kind of like a baptism. You're floating, peaceful. And it's wonderful.

"Your brain tells you that you can't do this, but the real you, the one below the thought process, knows you can. I came up and I floated, and I swam. The best part isn't actually doing it; it's the memory of it. It's how strong I feel after I'm done. And how I draw on that. I know I can let myself go. I didn't want to tell myself that I'm 'less than.' That I couldn't swim. That diminishes me. That makes me smaller.

"Am I really going to die with this fear in me, when I can take care of that? I don't want to look back at how I lived that way, and say, 'Why didn't I think I could zip wire, skydive, cliff dive?' That's what makes me feel great about doing it."

Anticipating terror is almost as bad as the terror itself. I remember losing it on a flume ride when I was twelve. As we climbed to the highest point of the ride, we stopped moving for a minute. My car was stalled at the very top, right next to a tiny booth. I could see the sheer drop below.

I had time to think, and to panic. I started pleading with the poor ride operator: "Please, please, let me get out. I don't want to go down. Please." That was the last roller-coaster ride of my life. But if I had Jan St. John's determination, I could be flying up and down with my arms in the air, screaming my head off, just like everyone else.

SNEAK BACKSTAGE

I f you always wanted to be a groupie but never made it past the twenty-ninth row, you might want to read Pamela Des Barres's classic tell-all *I'm with the Band* for inspiration. What a woman! In the '60s and '70s, Miss Pamela, as she was known, slept with half of the Rock and Roll Hall of Fame, including Jim Morrison, Jimmy Page, and Mick Jagger. Des Barres didn't have to sneak backstage—she lived there.

I didn't have to sneak there either. When Des Barres's book came out in 1987, I was a reporter for a trade magazine, covering music. I met a handful of stars, although the most intimate contact I had with them was a handshake. I drank at a table with Stephen Stills and Eric Burdon, chatted with Pete Townshend in a recording studio, and nearly burned down the Hard Rock Cafe in New York giving Robert Palmer a light.

Even more exciting, however, were the times I got to go backstage—at the Live Aid concert in 1985 and the Amnesty International concert the next year. These were all-day events televised around the world, so the "backstage" area was the size of a few football fields. There were satellite trucks and hospitality tents, endless food and drinks. There were roadies and marketing executives and reporters racing around. But there were very few musicians. Backstage wasn't about the stars; it was about the scene.

I haven't mingled with musicians since then, or even tried to, but many middle-aged women do (just ask Tom Jones). Celebrity lust doesn't end just because you turn forty. Elise Cannon, who's forty-six, has been sneaking backstage and hanging with the band since she was eighteen and went to the Whisky a Go Go on the Sunset Strip.

Cannon's first backstage mission was at a concert of the Who and the Clash at the Los Angeles Coliseum. "I saw a woman who had an all-area pass on her jeans, and she looked really drunk," she recalls. "I grabbed the pass from her pants and started running. Guess what was going on backstage? Nothing. There were big platters of food and no musicians. I just wanted to get a glimpse of the people I really cared about."

THE NEW CONCERT COUP

These days, instead of trying to snag an all-access pass, Cannon works different angles to get a set list. They're quite coveted, she says, because they're often handwritten. There's usually one by the drummer, and one on the floor near the lead singer's feet.

Cannon used to jump onstage and dance with bands, and at concerts now she still heads straight for the stage, no matter where her seats are. "I always want to stand in front of the band. I want to be surrounded by the music and have a connection," she says.

Cannon's tastes and tactics have changed over the past twenty-five years. Her favorite live band is Wilco, and she tries to arrange her business trips so she can catch as many of their shows as possible. Instead of infiltrating backstage now, Cannon tries to find out where the band members are going to be after the show. "You can find out where the band is hanging out just by asking the guys who sell the T-shirts," she says. Or the bouncers, who work for the venue, not for the band.

In 2006, after a show at the Ryman Auditorium in Nashville, Cannon went to a bar where the entire band was drinking. It was St. Patrick's Day. "There were three guys in there that had done the same thing," she says. "They were like teenage girls, they were so excited."

SPELUNK

There's a big difference between caverns and caves, and if you don't know what it is, you'll be thrown out of the next spelunkers' convention you attend. A cave is a large, naturally hollowed-out place in the ground, or in rock above the ground, that can be reached by land or by water. And a cavern is a cave with lights where park rangers take large groups of tourists in sneakers to see rock formations smudged with handprints.

Spelunking is defined as natural-cave exploration, with the emphasis on "exploration." It involves crawling on your hands and knees, slithering on your belly, and scooting around on your butt inside wet, musty holes in the ground. Oh, and wearing a cool helmet with a headlamp.

It's dangerous, this spelunking business: The rocks are wet and slippery, and you're feeling your way around in the dark. If you're not careful, you can get disoriented, which is what happened in 2007 to three college students in Texas—all experienced spelunkers. They lost their bearings and got stuck in a twelve-thousand-foot-long cave for thirty-two hours before they were rescued.

The danger and difficulty of caving make it an ideal sport for someone like Valerie Cranston, an avid hiker and adventure seeker. Cranston, who's sixty and lives near Carlsbad, New Mexico, went spelunking for the first time when she was forty-five. She happened to meet an experienced caver at a social event, and when he asked if she wanted to explore one of the local caves with him, she jumped at the chance.

"I always like the unknown," says Cranston. "I never put any limitations on myself. And I don't give up."

Her friend lent her a hat and a light, and Cranston brought her own lunch. Crouching, they entered the cave along with a handful of other spelunkers. Once they moved away from the entrance, they were in complete darkness, feeling their way through tiny passages.

It took a few hours for the spelunkers to get to the main room—a secret spot sealed off by rocks that someone in their group had to move. Inside, nobody said a word.

"There were these delicate sugar-crystal formations; it was like you were in a fantasy land," says Cranston. "Everyone was taking it in. The crystals were amber and a light pinkish-rose. . . . It was just astounding. We sat in that room for forty-five minutes. You just sit there in awe, almost having an out-of-body experience."

The most fabulous thing she's ever seen is El Capitan trail in New Mexico's Guadalupe Mountains National Park. First runner-up? That secret room in that first natural cave she visited.

"When you're on a mountain and you've got this vista, you're at the mercy of your environment," Cranston says. "Down underground, I feel like that environment is at the mercy of us. We could have destroyed it when we were in there. You have to respect the very fragile nature of those formations. It's a privilege to even set eyes on them."

39. SPELUNK

CREATE A
SACRED SPACE

I n the 1945 movie *A Place of One's Own,* the place in question is a haunted mansion in the English countryside. Memorable title, but nothing you'd wish for in your own life. In Michael Pollan's memoir *A Place of My Own,* the place is a hut in the woods that he builds as a personal sanctuary. That's more like it. He writes, "I wanted not only a room of my own, but a room of my own making. I wanted to build this place myself."

Perhaps you'd like to do the same: Create a sacred space that you can retreat to for solace, solitude, and spiritual connection.

Your reason for creating one is undoubtedly personal (isn't that the point?) and unique to your own circumstances. But the one thing that all sacred spaces have in common is their purpose: They allow you to be alone with your feelings. They're not sacred if your spouse, children, or plumber intrude, so if you live with other people, you may have to reserve time when you can be left completely alone.

Sacred spaces can occupy a large piece of real estate—a house, a room, or a clearing in the woods behind your back yard. More often than not, however, your corner of the universe is literally that: a nook or cranny somewhere in your home; a cozy area for your thoughts and prayers, and the things you put there to help preserve them.

Jo Donaldson's sacred space occupies a room in her house that contains her office furniture and a guest bed. It's basically a wicker night table in the corner that she's covered with all kinds of personal artifacts. She created it when her twenty-eight-year-old son, her only child, shipped out to Iraq.

"It was really the terror of losing him, and the desolation of him being gone, that made me do it," says Donaldson, who's now sixty. "I decided that I wanted a place that I could associate with him, and where I could pray for him. I figured that was the best way to keep him safe."

Here's what she arranged on the table:

- Her favorite picture of her son when he was little
- The tetherball trophy he won in third grade
- A Yankee candle
- An NIV (New International Version) bible
- A book of scriptures for mothers
- A cross

The cross has its own story. Donaldson had bought it three years earlier, while vacationing with a girlfriend in France. The trip itself was special; Donaldson's sole purpose was to spend two weeks combing the flea markets of Provence. One day Donaldson spotted a crucifix, meant to look like it was made of gold, which supposedly came from an ancient Catholic sect. Donaldson isn't Catholic, but, as she puts it, "who cares?" It spoke to her, and she took it home.

"I do believe in the power of prayer," she says. "I have not exercised it like I could have or think I should have. Someone once told me, 'When disaster strikes, it's not the time to introduce yourself to God, because it takes a while.'"

Donaldson makes time every day to sit in her sacred space in the spare room and pray for her son. Some days it's for only a few minutes; other days it's for much longer. "I know he's near the Turkish border, and when I see that things are blowing up there, I spend more time," she says. "Sometimes I spend all night there."

41

LEARN TO SAIL

If you haven't figured this out on your own yet, let me be the one to tell you: You'll never be captain of your own destiny. First mate, maybe, but you can steer things only so far before fate takes the wheel. You'll probably never be a captain of industry, either: Women head less than 3 percent of Fortune 500 companies. And even if you've been in the navy for twenty years, you're not likely to become the captain of your own vessel: Of the 51,000 women that the U.S. Navy employs, only 381 are captains. However, you *can* learn to skipper a twenty-foot yacht, which is a lot more relaxing than all of the above.

I get seasick, so bouncing on the waves would never be my dream come true, but in a way, I wish it were. I can picture myself on deck in a white button-down shirt with the sleeves rolled up, khaki shorts, and a pair of turquoise Crocs. (In my vision, I also have long, tanned legs, green eyes, and a dirty-blond ponytail.) The idea of sailing the ocean blue on a sunny day with a light breeze is enticing, even if the reality is nauseating. I might be able to handle a Sunfish on a lake somewhere, but the effect isn't the same.

Elise Cannon, who's forty-six, grew up at the beach, loves the ocean, and has even taken up surfing (see "Learn to Surf" on page 32) in recent years—and she still got seasick on her first ocean voyage. In 2008, she spent four days on a forty-eight-foot boat with a friend who was sailing from San Francisco to Mexico. For the first twenty-four hours, she had to sit on the top deck and stare at the horizon until the seasickness passed. After that, she had such a good time spotting dolphins, steering the boat, and being on watch at night that she's thinking of taking a small-craft sailing class.

"It's incredibly clean and fresh, and there's a feeling of fluidity," Cannon says. "It's like you're experiencing gravity in a different way. It's so exciting to be out there; it really is you versus nature. Is there anything as powerful and unpredictable as the ocean? There's a thrill in knowing that you're powerless."

Liz Becker is also well familiar with the thrill of sailing. She became a skipper when she was thirty-one, but skippered a yacht herself only three times. "It scared the bejesus out of me because I'd always sailed with men," she says. "I was never in charge. I'm qualified on paper."

Now, at forty-three, Becker is planning to get requalified. "I'm really nervous. I sail well enough, so I don't want anyone to judge me. It's a fairly large piece of equipment. You need to have sailing skill and understand your boat and your conditions. I kind of feel like I'm starting from scratch."

Becker's husband sails, so she could always just rely on him. But that's not what she wants. "My objective is to be able to take out groups of girlfriends," she says. "It would be nice to be at his level. The only way I'm going to be able to do that is to take the lessons by myself. I just don't want to be a passenger."

done

TAKE UP AN INSTRUMENT

The similarities abound: Two middle-aged women from different parts of the country decide to take piano lessons. Both have husbands who play instruments. Both play "Ode to Joy" for their families on Christmas. And both end up losing their piano teachers and aren't sure they'll continue. But the most significant thing they have in common is that neither one of them played an instrument as a child.

At our age, the activities we choose to try tend to fall into one of two categories: things we can do only in adulthood, and things we wish we had done in childhood. For example:

ADULTHOOD	CHILDHOOD
Strip (see page 22)	Tap-dance
Learn trapeze (see page 64)	Ride a bike
Record a song (see page 72)	Take piano lessons
Skydive (see page 116)	Dive off a high dive

Taking music lessons is a rite of passage for many children. If you weren't one of them, you really missed out—or so you've thought for the last forty or so years. To finally join that club is an exciting prospect . . . and a total unknown. What if you can't read music? What if you can't find the right key/chord/hole? What if you don't like playing? There's no instant gratification with this one; learning an instrument takes time, patience, and money. But what an accomplishment if you can do it! Our two middle-aged women are still trying.

Woman number one, Barbara Critchlow, was already taking boxing and Pilates lessons when she added piano to the list in 2007. Her husband plays the saxophone, her son is learning the trumpet, and Critchlow, who's fifty, thought she should try to do something musical. Her teacher made it as simple as possible, but after mastering "Twinkle, Twinkle, Little Star," Critchlow started to struggle with reading notes on the scale. Still, when her parents were over during Christmastime, she played "Ode to Joy."

"I could play a few notes on the piano," she says. "I was very proud of myself." But lately, Critchlow's been avoiding it. "I can't seem to make it a routine," she says, knowing that's just an excuse.

Woman number two, Debbie Vignovich, has stuck with it longer. She never imagined she'd do anything musical in her life, because she's almost tone-deaf. "That was something the other kids did," she says. "I always wanted to be in the glee club, but I couldn't sing the notes. I can't even hear the 'Happy Birthday' song. Stuff that had music in it wasn't going to be my thing."

Then, in 2006, an old friend with whom Vignovich had lost touch was widowed. Vignovich and a group of women got together and took some food to the friend's house, and while Vignovich was there, she noticed two pianos. She asked if the friend would consider giving her lessons. Two years later, Vignovich has a little repertoire.

"I can play the *New World Symphony* and I can almost play 'The Sting,' and I can play 'Ode to Joy,' which I later learned every seven-year-old knows how to play," says Vignovich, who's fifty-eight. "I feel very cocky that I can play the 'Happy Birthday' song when anybody has a birthday and tickled that I can play 'Heart and Soul,' like everyone else I knew in school.

"Everyone tells me how good I am. I think I'm going to have a recital for myself. I'll just invite my girlfriends, and have wine and cheese, and play the two songs I know. I think Bastille Day would be a good time."

LEAVE YOUR MARRIAGE

Even under the best of circumstances, ending a marriage is hard. But you know doing it is a good thing when your heart sings the minute you sign the papers. Any flavor of crappy marriage—abusive, nasty, empty, corrupt—robs you of the ability to really live. Every day you spend in one is less happy, less productive, and less peaceful than it could have been.

This isn't to say that all bad marriages should end. Circumstances change, people change, and marriages can change, too. Many factors can keep you from leaving: finances, fear, personal beliefs, and, above all, children. But when you do the math, and the plusses far outweigh the minuses, breaking away could be the best thing you ever do.

Debbie Caldwell lived through years of verbal abuse before finally and carefully ending her sixteen-year marriage when she was forty-one. "I woke up one morning just knowing I had to do it. I actually allowed that thought to be conscious. I went to a therapist. He said, 'How can I help you?' And I said, 'I think my marriage is over.'"

Caldwell spent more than a year deciding if, and how, she was going to leave. She read *The Good Divorce* and other books, determined to create the happiest ending possible for herself and her young children. She even went to marriage counseling as a last-ditch effort. "I just couldn't imagine that I could do it. I thought I would feel like a real loser, with a scarlet letter *D* on my chest," says Caldwell. "I was horrified at the thought of being a divorced person." One day during her deliberations, she went to a school fair and took notice of all the married couples. "I

THE LIST

thought, *I'm not going to be in this club anymore.* "Or have the third child she'd always wanted.

But on the day of her divorce, Caldwell felt incredibly relieved. She sold her house and bought a smaller one around the corner, while her husband moved to an apartment nearby. "It's so awesome to come home now," she says. "I go to sleep feeling safe in a way I haven't in years. It's peaceful, and I love the idea that I can create peace for my kids."

Caldwell got the canopy bed she'd always wanted. She discovered her high school pom-poms and hung them in her office. She painted her kitchen green. She took tennis lessons and joined the gym. (For the first time in her life, she wanted people to look at her.) She landed a high-profile job and became very serious about her finances—about providing for her children and for her own future. "I had been this adventurous, powerful girl," she says. "When I was married, I was always pulling him along. After the divorce, I came to fully embrace my power."

Caldwell wanted a good divorce, and that's what she got. She talks to her ex every day about parenting matters—and other things. They were married for half their lives, after all, and have a lot of memories and gossip to share. He has a girlfriend, and Caldwell has sown some wild oats. "I would love to be in a relationship," she says. "I love men. But not at all costs."

My Company Inc.

Me
PRESIDENT & CEO

START YOUR OWN BUSINESS

Real life throws you enough crap to dodge, delegate, or deal with that you don't need any more from your boss. You're an adult, for goodness' sake. You shouldn't have to grovel for a day off, or take on the work of three other people just because they all quit and the company's too cheap to replace them and it's dumped everything on you without forking over one extra dime. Plus, the snack machine's been broken for six months.

Working for the Man can really stink. So why don't *you* become the Man, so to speak?

Hating your job isn't the only reason to start your own business. Maybe you're looking to reenter the workforce, or want to have an income after you retire. Or perhaps, for a change, you want to do something you're really passionate about. This idea was one of Suzy Sands's main motivators. She was a freelance graphic designer for years, but after 9/11, when her design work dropped off significantly, she decided to turn her love of gardening into her livelihood. At age fifty-five, she opened a landscape design firm.

She went to the county courthouse to file a DBA (doing business as), got a license from the Texas State Department of Agriculture to buy plants wholesale, and jumped in. "I try to focus on urban-wildlife gardening," she says. "I'm trying to get people to think about enjoying nature in an urban setting, using native plants and natural pest management."

Sands worked full-time in the business for two and a half years, until an art director job came along that was too good to turn down.

Now she does landscaping on weekends, but she plans to return to it full-time in another nine years—when she's seventy. "I'll have nine more years of study and practice. Gardening is something people respect, and you are revered for knowledge and age. I think it's something you can grow old doing."

So what, exactly, is holding you back from starting your own business? Fear? Lack of control? Lack of funds? These are real concerns, but they don't have to be deal breakers. Let's tackle them one by one:

- **I'm afraid of failing.** (Translation: I'm afraid of losing my shirt.) The simple answer is, position yourself so you won't. Determine how much money you need—and double it. And ascertain how much money you already have—in savings, capital, and loans. Most important, decide how much money you're willing to lose before you pack it up and find a job.

- **I hate uncertainty.** Who doesn't? Predictability equals comfort. It can also equal boredom, frustration, and resentment. Are you really so rigid that you can't handle a few twists and turns? You can practice living with uncertainty by starting your business while still working your day job, if that's possible.

- **I don't have the money.** Unless you've been saving up since your first allowance, you'll have to get a loan. Some people go to friends and family members, but that's dicey. A safer bet is taking out a small-business loan. Two places to look: your local business development corporation, and banks that offer loans through the federal government's Small Business Administration.

There are lots of support and resources out there for women entrepreneurs. So, what do you think? Are you going to try to follow your dreams or let them pass?

ASK SOMEONE OUT

I f you're in the habit of making the first move, you don't need to read this. And you probably don't get why anyone else does, either. What's the big deal? If you meet someone you'd like to go out with, you just open your mouth and ask.

Sounds great. But if you've never been able to work up the nerve to ask someone out, you don't need criticism; you need help getting over your hurdles. And what might those be?

Check the ones that apply to you:

- I'm too shy.
- I'm afraid of rejection.
- I lack confidence.
- I'm afraid of rejection.
- I feel too pushy.
- I'm afraid of rejection.

Maybe if you knew what to say, you wouldn't be so afraid. This is foreign territory for you, after all. So, as a foreigner, you might pay a visit to the BBC's World Service/Learning English web pages, where you'll find a how-to section that offers both audio and written instruction in asking someone out. (The quickest method is to do a Google search for "BBC Ask Someone Out," and click on the first link that comes up. You can either hear the dialogue or read the script) If it works for non–English speakers, it could work for you. Here's a sample lesson:

WILLIAM: Hello there and welcome to another exciting install-ment of How To. My name is William Kremer. Now, in a previous ep-isode we looked at how to chat someone up—that is, how to talk to someone you don't know in a way that might make that person interested in you . . . in a romantic way. Well, now let's imagine that you've been chatting to this person, and you've managed to get him or her interested, so now it's time to ask him or her out. On a "date"? Well, saying "Will you come on a date with me?" is really too formal for English-speaking countries. Putting it like that is very embarrassing! Let's hear a more natural way of doing it. Susie and Mark work together, but they don't know each other that well.

SUSIE: I was thinking . . . do you want to meet up for a drink sometime?
MARK: Er . . . yeah, could do . . .
SUSIE: Just a beer after work or something.
MARK: Yeah—that would be nice. . . . Erm, let me see, I'm free tomorrow . . . or maybe Thursday.
SUSIE: No—tomorrow's good for me.
MARK: Okay—great!

Pretty simple, huh? Susie wasn't pushy, and Mark wasn't put off by her directness. (Would you have been if someone had approached you that way?) If for some crazy reason he had been, he might have turned her down. But do you think he would have been rude about it? Or would he have said something like "Er, um, I am so swamped with work right now, I'm not making any plans. Maybe when things lighten up . . . "?

That's not so awful, is it? Would you really pass up an opportunity to meet someone great for fear of hearing that? The only difference be-tween you and women who do the asking is that they don't take rejec-tion personally.

"I would feel like he has his reasons," says Anna Melillo, who's fifty-seven. "Maybe I'm not his type, or he has a wife or girlfriend. But he wouldn't have spent three hours of his evening talking with me if he didn't like me or find something enjoyable about me. My ego's not that delicate."

done

MAKE OVER
A ROOM

How much would you give to be on one of those reality TV shows on which you take the dog out for a ten-hour walk and come back to find your home totally redone? (Oh my god, I can't *believe* it!) You'd get brand-new everything, except for a few pieces with sentimental or aesthetic value that the team would work into the decorating scheme. New colors, textures, fabrics, and doodads—the designers would know your exact taste, even if you didn't. How great would that be?

Well, don't hold your breath. But also don't wait to totally transform one room in your house. Remaking a room is a quick, easy fix whenever you get antsy for a change. You can spend a lot of, or very little, money doing it, but either way, it's a small price to pay for having a new and energizing dwelling place, instead of staring at the same four walls for another twenty years.

Any decorator or stylist will tell you that the cheapest, most effective way to make over a room is to change the wall color. Choose something that's totally different from what's there now: Go soft and warm if you've had dark colors, or bright and bold if the room is muted. For an extra kick, pick colors you normally shy away from. You might be more flexible than you think.

Once you've painted, you can focus on accent pieces. A few choice purchases can have a big impact. Buy a large, inexpensive framed print that will dominate the wall and create a focal point for the room. Conversely, take much of the existing artwork and stick it somewhere else (the closet, perhaps?). Pick up some throw pillows that don't totally match—or that clash with—the other patterns or textures in the room. You want to mix it up a little bit. And add at least one noticeable new item to the room: an inexpensive wicker chair, a bookcase, a set of table lamps. Or go hog wild and buy all new stuff.

Room makeovers are great boredom busters, and they're also great milestone markers. When there's a change in your life, you want to define it and make it your own. Redecorating can accomplish that goal for you. For example, the minute Lisa Solod's husband moved out of their house, the furniture delivery truck pulled in. Within a week, she had converted their old bedroom into her own private beach house.

After she painted the bedroom and bathroom walls turquoise, here's what Solod bought for her new room:

- A sleigh bed
- Pictures featuring an ocean motif
- Blue and white voile drapes
- A blue and white striped chair and ottoman
- Fluffy white rugs
- White side tables with blue knobs
- Pillows and more pillows
- Blue vases and white silk flowers

"I went a little nuts," says Solod, who's fifty-two. "It was really a way to stop one part of my life and start another. I could do it exactly how I wanted it without clearing it with anyone. I had wanted to live by the beach for thirty years. You wouldn't even know it was the same room; it was absolutely beautiful."

HIRE A PERSONAL SHOPPER

The one and only time I used a personal shopper, I was in my mid-thirties and desperate. My editor was sending me to Nashville to attend a symposium held by Vice President Gore—with only two days' notice. I had a one-year-old baby whom I was nursing at the time, which is to say that I didn't have any decent business clothes that still fit. So I called the personal shopping service at Saks Fifth Avenue, told them my size and what I needed, and ran the eight blocks from my office to the store.

> **"I like my money right where I can see it: hanging in my closet."**
>
> —Carrie on *Sex and the City*

When I arrived, a shopper—my shopper—was waiting for me with a dressing room full of clothes. Within five minutes I had run through all of them; the shopper put them back on hangers as fast as I took them off. Once she saw my body in person, she went running back to the floor for different cuts and sizes. It was like having a very efficient, nonjudgmental mom in the dressing room with me.

After twenty minutes, I had a pale green Michael Kors suit—reduced, reduced, reduced—and a pair of black pumps (yes, she ran down to the shoe department, too). My shopper even arranged for the suit to be altered overnight. What did I pay for this fabulous service? Absolutely nothing. Department stores actually give it away.

Judy Tiano, meanwhile, paid $600 for a private personal shopper, but that was a different situation. Tiano, who's forty-six, was a fan of the reality show *What Not to Wear,* on which two fashion gurus make over people's wardrobes and show them how to make the best of their big butt/small boobs/short waist. At five-foot-eight and 120 pounds, Tiano didn't need to hide anything. She just wanted help finding a style that worked for her. A grown-up style.

"I could wear a short skirt and it looked great, but it didn't feel right," she says. "It didn't seem appropriate. It's the age thing. What is appropriate over forty?"

> **"Whoever said money can't buy happiness simply didn't know where to go shopping."**
>
> —Bo Derek

Tiano called the mall and got the name of a personal shopper. They talked over the phone about sizes and styles, then arranged to meet at the mall. The shopper had already gone to a number of stores and pulled merchandise she thought Tiano might like. She was right more often than she was wrong. Tiano bought items she never would have considered on her own, including a $200 pair of jeans at Armani.

"They were more than I've ever paid for a pair of jeans, but I still have them and still like them," she says. "I look smoking in those jeans. The shopper taught me something: You invest in clothes that are really good. You think about the cost per wear and measure them by usefulness, not dollars."

Tiano walked out that day with bags of clothes, shoes, and accessories, having spent so much (about $3,000) that her credit card companies suspected fraud and cut her off. "I figured if I was spending all this money on the shopper, I'd better make it worth it by buying a lot of stuff."

MAKE A BIG MOVE

In the summer of 2007, my friend Louise moved from the suburbs of New York City to Santa Monica, California, with a month's notice. In that time, she rented out her four-bedroom home near the Long Island Sound and signed a lease on an apartment a block and a half from the Pacific Ocean. She packed up all her belongings while packing her twins off to college. Then she and her husband boarded a plane and left their old lives behind.

The timing was both crazy and perfect. They were about to be empty-nesters, and nothing was tying them to New York anymore. Their oldest daughter was at college in Pittsburgh; Louise's sister was in Dayton and her brother was in southern New Jersey; and her father, who had lived outside Philadelphia, had died earlier in the year. Louise and her husband would be leaving friends, but many had already left them to make their own empty-nest moves.

The surprise for Louise, who's fifty-five, wasn't that she went, but how quickly she decided to go. They'd been talking about moving after the twins left home—to Boston, maybe, or Washington, D.C. Then her husband got a job offer and presented a very different option: What would she think of moving to Los Angeles . . . in a month?

"To my credit, I did not immediately say, 'Are you nuts?'" says Louise. "There are things you know in your blood and your cells that your mind never knew. I just had an overwhelming visceral reaction that was, *Yeah!* Living at the beach has been a lifelong dream. When this happened, I knew I had to do it."

Louise had lived in New York for twenty-three years, and in the last five had lost both of her parents and launched all three of her kids. "It was like, *My work is done,*" she says. "I wanted to get out of the competitive New York area. I wanted to not know everyone I saw at the supermarket."

After twenty years in the same house, Louise and her husband were surrounded by an overwhelming amount of stuff they didn't need. When they moved into their new apartment, Louise, who's a freelance writer, wanted to keep it spare and unencumbered—like her life suddenly was. "For the first week, I was just in the space and getting used to being very untethered—not in a bad way. I was learning the basics of driving in L.A., learning how to get where I had to go."

She began building a social life and discovered that it wasn't hard to do, even without kids to help make connections. "We knew one couple, and they invited us into their dinner circle. That's five couples right there," she says. "They seem to want to be making new friends; they're happy to have us as new blood." She also joined a writers' group and reconnected with a woman in her neighborhood whom she knew from New York. They now meet every Wednesday for a walk and lunch.

The trickier part is keeping up old friendships, and Louise spends Sunday afternoons on the phone. "I'm the one who made the choice to move; it's up to me to reach out," she says. Part of the cost of moving has been airfare—for Louise to see her sister; for the kids to come back and forth.

This move wasn't what Louise expected, but it's exactly what she wanted. "The ground is moving a bit underneath my feet," she says. "But it makes me feel young that I had the emotional wherewithal to embrace something new."

CONQUER A FEAR

I know a handful of women who are afraid to drive, although not in the same way. One hates driving in the city, one avoids local streets, and one dreads highways. Together, they could take a dandy road trip. But there's a fourth fearful woman I know who would never join them, because she panics whenever she's even sitting in a car that someone else is driving.

Years ago, I worked with a young woman who ate her liver out every time she got in an elevator—and we worked on the twenty-eighth floor, poor thing. My neighbor, I just discovered, is afraid of roller coasters (as am I), and my mother-in-law is frightened by fast and bumpy boat rides (ditto). Here's what else I'm scared of:

- Flying
- Getting mammograms
- Swimming in the ocean
- Driving through tunnels

I wish this weren't me.

It would be nice to get on a plane and watch the movie, for once, rather than clutching the armrests and squeezing my eyes shut (and that's *after* taking two sedatives). Or to go for a pleasure cruise on a beautiful summer day. But as much as I'd love to be free, I don't know how to ditch these fears of mine. So I relish the stories of women, like Spike Gillespie and Jan St. John, who've ditched theirs—one by accident, one on purpose.

Jan St. John went head to head with her fears the year she turned fifty-six, when she decided to challenge every expectation she had of herself. To that end, she dove off a cliff (more on that on page 90) and jumped out of a plane (page 116), and proved to herself that she was bigger and badder than the things that scared her.

Gillespie, forty-four, would still be a nervous wreck before boarding a plane if she hadn't had to confront a much bigger fear: being abandoned. When her second husband walked out on her in 2007, she was so devastated that she became physically ill and deeply depressed. Her friends responded by sending her on trips—about one per month, sometimes in small planes. "I thought, *Who cares if the plane crashes?*" says Gillespie. "It was a big, melodramatic response."

But truthfully, she wasn't scared to fly anymore. "The bottom line was that my biggest fear in life was being left, and I survived it," she says. "It was one of those transformations you'd see in the movies, this out-of-the-blue thing. It was like something was lifted from me."

That's cheating, you might say. Gillespie didn't really confront her fears; they just abandoned her without her knowing it. Maybe. But she took that experience and started slaying some of her other demons. She has a boyfriend now, and she doesn't want her fear of abandonment to mess things up. "It's very joyous but also extremely nerve-racking, because I'm waiting for him to leave," she says. "I can't give in to this fear, though. I make a conscious choice to respond to the facts: *No, look, he's here.*"

And if one day he isn't, Gillespie won't be devastated like she was when her husband jumped ship. "He might leave, but I can get through it."

I'd like to take a page from Gillespie's book and respond to the facts the next time I get on a plane: *Nothing's wrong. The pilots know what they're doing. And I've got a movie to watch.*

50

SKYDIVE

Jan St. John's skydiving story is inspiring—whether or not you'd ever consider jumping out of a plane. But if you're a woman with control issues, like St. John is, it's particularly powerful. Skydiving, after all, is the ultimate exercise in letting go, as you throw caution, and yourself, to the wind. It's also one of the most dramatic experiences imaginable. Really, what could be more intense than tossing yourself out of a plane?

For St. John, a fifty-six-year-old fitness instructor, going skydiving during Christmas break with her husband and two grown daughters capped off a year of change—a year in which she decided to push beyond her comfort zone and confront her fears.

"We all have a lifetime list of things we'd like to do; skydiving was always on my list," she says. "It is a terrifying thought because I'm terrified of heights. But I'm in the second half of my life, and at this stage, you're at a crossroads: Your life can get a little bit smaller, or it can get a little bit bigger. I wanted mine to get bigger.

"I really wanted to start exploring the opposites in myself. I always liked things to be in control; I was always waiting for the other shoe to drop. So I went on a quest for grace."

Christmas was always a big event at St. John's house, and that's exactly why she chose to give it up that year. She suggested to her family that they go away for the holiday instead, to a destination that would be the "opposite" of Christmas. Her daughters came up with

Vegas, and St. John knew immediately what they'd all be doing instead of carving the ham.

"We went out over the Hoover Dam, three miles up in the tiniest, scariest plane," she recalls. "I was the last one out. I saw my two daughters and my husband fall out of the plane, and it was every mother's worst nightmare. They were there one minute, and the next minute they'd disappeared completely.

"We did a tandem jump, meaning the instructor is on your back the whole time. I sat on the edge of the plane, with my feet hanging out over the side. He said, 'One, two, three,' and he threw me forward.

"I was free-falling through space; it was the longest minute of my life. The feeling is so crazy. You don't even get the sense that you're falling to the ground. When your chute goes up, it snaps you upward. The first thing I did when my chute went up was look for three other chutes. Then there were the four of us, just twirling and floating.

"I had this incredible sense of euphoria. The whole experience was so huge for something that only lasts around a half hour. It's life-changing in everything that it represents. You will be more frightened than you've ever been in your life. But that's what you came for. I feel like if I can do this, I can do anything."

HOW TO PICK A DROP ZONE

Skydiving instructors are not regulated by the federal government—only the pilots and the equipment are. That means you could go out tomorrow, buy some parachutes, and open your own drop zone without breaking any laws. The industry does have a self-policing group, called the United States Parachute Association (www.uspa.org), that has created safety guidelines and a voluntary certification program for drop zones. The group's website lists all of the certified drop zones by state, so you can at least know that those companies have agreed to follow industry standards.

EAT SOMETHING REALLY WEIRD

The grossest thing I never ate was sweetbreads, which my boss ordered for me at dinner one night in honor of the first anniversary of my brain surgery (long story). I was twenty-four. I'm not sure if he mistakenly thought sweetbreads were cows' brains, instead of their thymus, or if he knew they weren't brains, but just looked like they were—which is what mattered, anyhow.

Either way, when that plate hit the table, I almost hit the road. The sweetbreads loosely resembled a clump of fat worms—or a chunk of cerebellum. I gagged, my boss laughed, and I finished up with a nice steak and a truly memorable night out.

I'm embarrassed to say that I haven't broadened my culinary horizons much in the last two decades. If anything, I think I'm getting less adventurous. You know it's bad when your friend's son will eat, at age eleven, what you wouldn't touch at twenty-four, or even now.

Beth, who's forty-six, relays her story: "Last week we took the kids to Momofuku Noodle Bar in the East Village. Ben was cruising the menu and saw 'fried sweetbreads.' He asked to order it. I asked if he was sure; he said yes. Turns out, he thought it would be something like deep-fried cake, but instead it was yummy, crunchy, salty meat.

"By about two-thirds of the way through dinner, he had asked me what they were enough times that I told him: deep-fried adrenal glands from a young cow. He said, 'Okay,' and kept on eating. Not to be outdone, I ate some too. I have to say, it was a rush—like a dare. And they did taste great."

TASTES NOTHING LIKE CHICKEN

- *Balut* (Southeast Asia): fertilized duck egg with a partially formed duck fetus inside
- Haggis (Scotland): boiled sheep's stomach stuffed with minced sheep lung, heart, liver, and oatmeal
- Nutria, a.k.a. ragondin (Louisiana, by way of South America): lean red meat from an aquatic, plant-eating rodent
- Scrapple (United States): scraps of pig (such as lips, organs, and snout), mixed with cornmeal and flour and baked into a loaf
- *Criadillas* (Spain and Canada): bull testicles, fried, poached, or sliced and cooked with garlic and parsley

Yummy, crunchy, salty meat. Look what I missed out on.

Beth has eaten some pretty weird stuff without her kids, too. On a business trip to France once, she accidentally ate something she would never have ordered if she'd had a clue: slivered pig's ears in a sherry vinaigrette. Here's how that happened:

"One evening, after a program that ran very late, we were taken to the best regional restaurant in Angoulême. It was eleven when we sat down, and I was starving. We had a few aperitifs as we reviewed the menu, which definitely enhanced my French—so I thought. I saw a starter that I read as 'little birds in sherry vinaigrette.' So I ordered it.

"The order came, and it was very good. Lots of differently textured slivers—some salty and chewy, others that were spring onions. About halfway through, I asked our guide what kind of bacon I was eating; I wasn't used to this texture. She looked at me strangely and said, 'It is the ear.' I said, '*Pardon?*' She said again, 'The ear. Didn't you know?' I had confused *oreille* with *oiseau!*

"I have to say, though, I'm glad I ate it. I like being a risk-taker with food. Sometime I'll tell you about the kidneys in cream sauce with fresh-killed venison and homemade spaetzle. . . ."

BECOME A BARTENDER OR A SOMMELIER

Bartending may be the only profession in the world—other than the *oldest* profession in the world—in which you can go from novice to paid professional overnight, bringing home as much as $400 in cash after your first shift. All it takes is one week at a reputable bartending school, and you've got a career with plentiful jobs, flexible hours, and great camaraderie.

The American Bartenders School, which has five locations around the United States, offers ten four-hour classes for $889. Most students have a job within a few days of completing the course. "If you're going to work at the local bar, you don't need to go to school, but if you want to work in a decent place, you do," says instructor Jean Martinho. "Drinking is very sophisticated today."

Becoming a sommelier (wine steward) is a more rigorous process. If you make it to the top, you can earn a six-figure salary, but to get there, you'll need an extensive knowledge of wine and years of restaurant work under your belt. The Wine & Spirit Education Trust offers classes and certification in twenty locations. But you're not going to come out of school and get a job as a sommelier the next day. (A hostess, maybe.)

There are other ways to work with wine besides draping a napkin over your arm and pouring, however. Sue Guerra, who's forty-eight, traded a lucrative job in sales for work at an upscale wine shop, where she hauls cases, sells on the floor, and helps with tastings. "I was always interested in wine—the geography, the language, the potential for examining other cultures," says Guerra, who's forty-eight. "I took customers out to dinner who looked to me to understand the wine list. It was something I wanted to get to know."

Guerra started by taking an intermediate course at the International Wine Center in Manhattan; the class runs thirty-seven hours and costs $788. (The center also offers home-study programs.) Eventually, she got her advanced certification.

"At that level, it's not just about the wines; it's about the science, the regions, the climate, the laws, and what happens in the vineyard," Guerra says. "It's pretty intense. You learn about all the wine regions of the world, including some of the obscure ones, like Romania, Bulgaria, Hungary, and Greece. The exam is one hundred multiple-choice questions, short-answer questions, and a blind tasting. You have to describe the classification of all the German wines.

"I was still working a sixty-hour-a-week job. But I couldn't wait to spend my weekends studying for this wine class. At that point, the lightbulb went off and I started to think that this was a career plan."

Guerra gave six months' notice at work, reduced her hours, and began interviewing with wine distributors and sales reps. Ultimately, she decided to start at the wine store of a fellow International Wine Center graduate in her town. "My end game would be to work for an importer or distributor," she says. "My husband retired and went to culinary school, so maybe there's a joint venture in our future.

"Part of me says I wish I realized this when I was twenty; think of how much farther ahead I'd be. But I don't dwell on regret."

Hopefully you won't either.

TELL SOMEONE
TO SCREW OFF

God, it feels good. After putting up with somebody's rudeness, meanness, or hostility, telling them off is as satisfying as a pint of Häagen-Dazs Dulce de Leche. What makes us stay mute and suffer discomfort when someone is offensive? There's a good-girl component to it, no doubt, and a general desire to keep things pleasant and civil. But when other people are blowing their noxious fumes in your direction, life is already unpleasant.

Rochelle Jewell Shapiro, who's sixty, started telling people off in her forties, and she's never looked back. She sent me this story in an email:

I met this woman in a class given by the school psychologist at our children's middle school, and we became friends. Before long, she confided in me about a torrid affair she was having, going into great detail.

I really didn't want to hear about this. I felt bad for her husband and sons, whom I knew. "Go to therapy," I told her. She did, and she had an affair with the therapist that she had to tell me all about, including how his leather couch got stained and how they had to roll onto the floor so she could get her legs around his hips.

Listening to her on the phone one day, I realized that she was somehow foisting on me the role of a voyeur, that at least half her pleasure was telling all of this to me. I wanted out.

"Screw anyone you want," I said over lunch, when she started up again, "except for my husband, of course, but I don't want to hear another word about your affairs."

"But friends are supposed to be intimate," she argued.

"Just drop the subject," I insisted.

"I have to tell you one thing," she said dramatically. "He masturbates in front of me."

I got up from my chair and told her that she was now my former friend. When I walked out, I felt the first thrill since this whole sordid business began. She left messages on my phone that I never returned.

Delighted for Shapiro, I emailed her back:

I myself happen to be a serial victim of other women's indignation, usually because I took the parking space they wanted or didn't wait for them to pass first on a crowded sidewalk. I've had women give me the finger for such offenses.

I've always tried to get back in their faces, but I've only just had my first success. Normally they run away when you call them on it, but the other week, my aggressor was trapped.

I was meeting my friend Pat at Starbucks one afternoon. I arrived first and got in line. A woman walked in behind me, followed seconds later by Pat. I was ready to order and asked Pat what she wanted (it was my turn to buy, anyway), and then I told the cashier that I was ordering a drink for my friend, too.

The woman behind me said under her breath, with venom, "Of course you are."

I turned around and said, "Excuse me?"

She looked at me like a deer in headlights. "I didn't say anything."

I said calmly, "Of course you did."

She said nothing.

I continued, "Just so you can understand the situation, I was meeting my friend here, and it was my turn to pay. So I ordered for us both."

She said nothing.

I was elated because I had finally stuck it to one of these rude, self-righteous, judgmental bitches that can dish it out but not take it.

It feels good just talking about it.

TAKE SINGING LESSONS

How many of us deny a talent because we're too embarrassed to expose it, or suppress a passion because we're afraid to pursue it? Okay, how old are we?

This isn't the sixth-grade talent show. This is your life, and you can fill it with whatever you want—including a lot of unfulfilled promises you make to yourself. The women featured in this book will all tell you to seize the moment, and to not hold anything back. If you want to grab some guy and plant a wet one on him, go for it. (See "Kiss a Total Stranger" on page 136.) If you love to sing, then sing . . . or forever wish you had.

Don't worry, I'm getting off the soapbox now.

Singing is one of life's greatest joys—even if you can't carry a tune. If you have a good voice, singing lessons or classes can give you even more to rejoice about by taking your natural gift and expanding its range. You'll hear an improvement the minute you open your mouth. (If you go onto YouTube and pull up "Ellen DeGeneres voice lessons," you'll see what a few minutes with a coach did for her.) As with anything else, success breeds success and builds confidence. Who knows—you might feel so good about your singing that you'll let someone other than the dog hear you.

Is it too late to train your voice to do great things? You probably won't become a professional diva at this point. Opera singers usually start vocal training in their teens, although they often don't debut until their twenties. But there are always exceptions. Canadian singer Elaine

THE LIST

Brown (who also recorded her own CD—see "Record Your Own Music" on page 72) began taking voice lessons in 1997, at the same time her daughter did. Ten years later, at age fifty-eight, she competed on a television show called *Bathroom Divas: So You Want to Be an Opera Star?* She's been performing since then and has released a CD called *Elaine—Look at Me Now.*

Jody Bower had more modest aspirations when she started taking singing lessons at age fifty-one: She wanted to audition for a local singing group. The group's director is nationally known, and the admission standards are high. Bower didn't have the confidence to try without some instruction.

"I had sung in the alto section in choirs but never thought I had much of a voice," she says. "When I started lessons I struggled, for some time, to get over my shyness about singing by myself in front of other people. My teacher kept telling me I was holding back my voice and sabotaging myself.

"I found that the act of singing out loud in front of someone brought out all my insecurities and self-doubts, so I went for counseling. The counselor asked, 'How old is the girl who wants to sing?' I realized the girl who wanted to sing was about sixteen. When I was sixteen I was a very, very shy wallflower, longing to be noticed."

Once she began loosening up, Bower discovered that she has a powerful mezzo-soprano voice. She started singing in an elite choir and performing solos at church and in a concert series in her town. Now she's preparing for her first recital as a solo performer. "I love performing," she says. "I love my new identity as a singer. Singing lessons changed my life."

And you're still waiting?

SWITCH CAREERS/
GO BACK TO
SCHOOL

Some women rearrange the furniture once a year to keep things fresh and interesting. Others reinvent themselves, often by returning to school or switching careers. It's a rebirth of sorts: New worlds open up to you, and you to them.

Most of us are lucky—or daring—enough to start over once or twice in our lives, but there are always show-offs like Kit Bakke, who's on her fourth career, and Peggy Kass, who's on her fifth. What's with these women?

Well, they're both sixty-one. They both started out as nurses and ended up as writers. And they both have an appetite for change. But they made different decisions for different reasons along the way, as you'll learn.

When she was thirty-seven, Kass went to design school. At forty, she started her own lighting design firm. In just three years, working seventy hours a week, she reached her ultimate goal. "I did a high-end, multimillion-dollar house in Napa, California," she says. "I got the project done and I thought, *I did it perfectly.* Usually the perfect project is the next project."

Kass closed her business to spend more time with her husband and her two young sons, but within three years, she was divorced. She decided to get a college degree (her first) in English literature and try to become a technical writer. She was fifty-one—and nervous. Here's what happened next:

- She graduated summa cum laude at fifty-three and got a job as a technical editor and copy editor at a small publishing firm.
- When the boss from hell arrived, she quit and entered a master's program in English at fifty-six.
- She sold her house and moved a few hours north to attend school, leaving behind her sons and the community she'd lived in for twenty-eight years.
- She graduated at fifty-eight and spent a year working for the university, creating a writing program for faculty members.
- She traveled for the next two years, writing about her journey as she went.
- She returned, hired an agent, and is finishing up a memoir about her travels, kicking off her latest career as a writer.

"It takes a lot of courage and willingness to take risks," Kass says. "I was willing to use up my savings. I sold two houses and lived off the money. It may not work out, but you can't be afraid of failing."

When Kit Bakke turned fifty, she decided to test the theory that after a certain age, it's nearly impossible to change fields.

After working for years in the technology department of an HMO, she was tired of teamwork and having to rely on others. Bakke decided to try consulting, where she'd be measured by her own performance. Within months, she had an offer from a start-up firm owned by three guys in their late twenties who were looking to break into the health-care market. They hired her for her contacts and expertise.

It was a totally different world from the one Bakke was used to. She had an expense account and got big bonuses. "In 2002, I bought a BMW with my bonus," she says. "I was appalled at the thought that I even *wanted* a BMW!"

At fifty-six, Bakke took a one-year leave of absence to write a book, which she sold in 2004. Her advice on switching careers after age fifty: "Pretend age isn't an issue, and it won't be an issue."

LEARN TO BOX

Many women, including me, can't imagine throwing a punch. We didn't grow up having fistfights (unless it was with a sibling, which doesn't count), and we never take it outside when we argue with someone. But just because we don't punch doesn't mean we wouldn't like to. Really, who wouldn't enjoy pounding the crap out of something once in a while?

Boxing gives you that release. It allows you to feel your power and show your strength without holding anything back. It builds muscles and confidence. And if you're as lucky as Sue Ostfield was, it allows you to have close physical contact with really handsome men. Here's how it happened:

The summer before last, Ostfield was invited to a bizarre book promotion in New York City. The main event was a three-round boxing match between authors Jonathan "The Herring" Ames and Craig Davidson at the legendary Gleason's Gym in Brooklyn, followed by a postfight party at a bar. At the party, Ostfield, who's forty-four, met a cute guy who turned out to be Ames's trainer. He gave her his phone number in case she ever wanted to take boxing lessons. Until that night, she wouldn't have considered it.

Six months later, Ostfield was delayed returning home from a business trip. Her plans for the night were ruined, and she felt very sorry for herself. On the cab ride from the airport, she spotted a sign for Gleason's in the distance, and when she got home—at ten o'clock at night—she called the cute trainer and scheduled a lesson for the following Saturday morning.

"I didn't know what to expect," says Ostfield. "When I showed up at the gym, I was the only woman, and the guys there had metal on their teeth. I was just trying to keep under the radar and not make a fool out of myself. The next time, I realized that there were other women—some serious boxers and some checking it out, like I was."

Ostfield went every Saturday morning for the next few months. "At first it was a challenge to think I could do the workout at all," she says. "I was never great at jumping rope, but I had a natural left hook."

Over time, Ostfield's arms bulked up and her tummy flattened. The changes felt age-defying. But one day at the gym, a woman who was preparing for the Golden Gloves competition asked the trainer if Ostfield was "the new girl." That's when Ostfield realized that her trainer had grander aspirations for her than she wanted. Since she didn't want to fight in the ring, she hung up her gloves. But boxing's benefits stayed with her. It made her tough in more ways than one. She no longer beats around the bush or shies away from saying difficult things. "It's helped me to not pull any punches with people," she says.

Ostfield's mother can attest to that. One day in December 2007, the two of them were out driving together. The roads were slippery, and Ostfield told her mother to switch into second gear to get more traction. Her mother was so distracted looking at the gears that she didn't notice that the car in front of them had slowed down. Without thinking, Ostfield yelled, "You're going to get us killed!" and punched her mother in the arm. Seems as if the training was good for her reflexes—and pulling quick punches. Even unintentional ones.

Done

GET A MAKEOVER

When I was in my twenties, I colored my hair every six weeks, just for kicks. It was jolly good fun because I left it up to the hairstylist to cook up a new formula every time. What did I care if it came out bright red? I didn't worry about makeup in those days, either; I had nice, young skin. I just washed my face, grabbed my lip gloss, and went.

The older I get (I'm forty-six), the more time and money I spend on maintenance. I have a bathroom drawer stocked with anti-aging creams and gels. Every few months, I put subtle highlights in my hair to add some life to it—not to camouflage grays yet, but that's coming. And every day I put on a full face of makeup, even if my only outing is to the drugstore. Trying to sustain the status quo is like a second job.

CHEEK TECHNIQUE

To put on powdered blush, smile and apply blush to the apples of your cheeks with a makeup brush. From there, brush all the way back to your ear. Then blend with little downward strokes back to your cheeks.

When I started writing this book, I thought I might want to try a makeover myself. Why not? It would be fun. By the time I finally got one, I was champing at the bit. I didn't just want a better me—I wanted a brand-new me. And someone else could figure out what that was. Surprise me.

I decided to start by changing my hair. I made an appointment at a trendy salon on Manhattan's east side, right around the corner from Bloomingdale's. Two hours before my cut, I went to the Bobbi Brown counter, where they do makeovers anytime without an appointment. In less than five minutes, I got my surprise.

Kimberly, the makeup artist, started my makeover with a skin-care routine: cleanser, toner, "multibenefit" serum, moisturizer, and eye cream. When she was done, my skin was soft and bright. It was like being twenty-five again. I actually saw a new me in the mirror—and it was the *old* me.

She moved on to foundation, concealer, bronzer, blush, eye shadow, gel eyeliner, mascara, and this very cool eyebrow shaper that colors your brows. At the end, I thought I looked very pretty and natural. But the thrill of feeling naturally pretty had come long before then. Less, in this case, was much, much more.

Around the corner, at the Mark Garrison salon, I sat waiting to hear what my stylist—Mark Garrison himself—had in mind for me. Something really bold, I imagined, judging from the pictures on his website. I was a bit disappointed to hear that he wouldn't change the length much, and that the color could be lighter, but not too much lighter. Then, halfway through the cut, he said, "You've got really good texture," and when I looked in the mirror, I saw a hairstyle that I hadn't seen on me for decades: chin-length, layered, wavy. It had happened again: The new me was the old me.

For days, I marveled at my new/old caramel-colored curls as if they were some kind of miracle. (The real miracle is the $30 Kérastase Oléo-Curl Definition Cream by L'Oréal that I bought at the salon.) I don't do anything to my hair, other than rub in the cream. And I've stopped wearing eye shadow and eyeliner every day (although I do put on foundation and a dusting of bronzer). Getting ready in the morning is almost as quick as it was when I was twenty-five. And now I appreciate it.

BUY SOMETHING OUTRAGEOUSLY EXPENSIVE

Extravagance is a relative thing: One woman's impulse buy can be another woman's down payment on a condo. But the thrill of splurging—particularly on oneself—is absolute. Paying a crazy amount of money for something, whether it's a bottle of perfume or a luxury sedan, can be intoxicating.

Five hundred dollars for a Prada Tessuto soft calf satchel? You wouldn't spend it every day, but if that bag is what makes your pulse quicken and your eyes light up, there are good reasons to go for it.

- You deserve it.
- It's stupid to wait forever.
- You can't spend every day of your life being prudent. Sometimes you've got to be a little reckless.

Barbara Goldberg waited forty-eight years to indulge, until a moment arrived that was so worth celebrating, it also merited splurging. Her husband, a journalist, was invited to the annual White House press dinner, and she was going with him. They'd be staying overnight in a Washington hotel—alone. Her husband was excited, which made it all the more exhilarating for her to drop $350 on a bra-and-panties set that cost six times as much as the dress she was planning to wear over it.

For her big purchase, Goldberg went to an old-fashioned foundations store in Manhattan and put herself in the hands of trained professionals—literally. "The saleswomen scoop up your boobs and put them into the cups," says Goldberg. "When do you get service like that?" Still, when she saw the price tag, she had to stop and justify the expense in her own mind.

It wasn't hard.

"I have a challenging job," says Goldberg, a media specialist at a healthcare public relations firm. "I work hard every day. I wasn't blowing someone else's money. I don't treat myself very often, and I deserve it."

Infrequency is the trick to these treats; the minute they become a regular thing, they lose some of their luster. A few years ago, my friend Aviva, who's thirty-eight, blew $250 in holiday gift cards on makeup and was giddy about it for days.

"I never spend money on myself like that," she says. "I don't get massages or facials or manicures and pedicures. I don't do spa days with my girlfriends, mainly because I'd feel guilty spending the money."

Cosmetics were the perfect indulgence because they gave Aviva a chance to do something she rarely can: buy the very best. "I could never afford the new 'it' handbag and boots, but I can afford the new 'it' makeup," she explains. "For a mere $250, I am wearing *the* best makeup that money can buy."

Aviva's holiday binge has become a tradition. Every year she takes the gift cards she gets from her parents and father-in-law and treats herself to trendy, top-of-the-line cosmetics. She looks forward to her annual spree—throughout the year, she clips magazine articles touting certain concealers or mascara—even though it doesn't feel quite as decadent as it did the first time. Still, it's a reminder that every once in a while, she deserves the best.

What about you?

ESCAPE
(FOR THE DAY,
WEEKEND, OR WEEK)

Among the many insights that mothers, therapists, and tarot card readers like to offer is this nebulous observation: "You're not running toward something, you're running away from something." They say it as if it's a bad thing, which it's not. In the same way that absence makes the heart grow fonder, escaping your everyday life makes you appreciate it more when you're back—or at least accept it with a better sense of humor.

I've broken loose many times. In fact, I try to make a habit of it. Twice while writing this book, I left my family for a few days so I could work without distraction. I checked into an inn at the beach and never left my room, except to get coffee from the breakfast room and sandwiches from the deli down the street.

I did it for work. But I loved it for myself. Four days with nobody to talk to, argue with, bribe, browbeat, or make lunch for. No walking the dog or loading the dishwasher or checking the mail. Beyond that, when I left home, I had no idea what to expect. Everything was an unknown: how my room would look, whether the local pizza place delivered, what the afternoon cookie assortment would be. It was just great to be somewhere different—and far, far away from day-to-day life.

Escape is a state of mind, not a destination, but it can be more exotic than a couple of nights locked in a hotel room with a laptop and some Danishes. My friend Jackie, for example, decided to leave her family for a long weekend to visit her college roommate in Aspen. She booked her flight the minute her husband told her he'd be taking two business trips for a total of five weeks, leaving her alone with three children. Boy, was she out of there.

On Jackie's second day in Aspen, she and her old roommate escaped from the roommate's daily grind to go cross-country skiing in a Colorado state park. In the middle of the park, accessible only on foot or skis, was a lodge. The two runaways stopped there for a big lunch and a glass of wine.

"It was absolutely beautiful," says Jackie, who's forty-two. "It was just the two of us. I never could have done that with three kids around. When we were on the trails, we were the only ones around."

I learned long ago the value of finding mini-escapes that are, at most, an hour away. Depending on where you go, even a half-day getaway can restore you. Periodically, I take friends to the Italian section of the Bronx, where the smell of fresh-baked bread fills the street, and the lines at the mozzarella store extend to the sidewalk. When people in the markets argue in Italian, I know I'm someplace different. People I bring for the first time always feel like they've been to Italy for three hours.

Every now and then, my neighbor and I cross two bridges to get to the Greek neighborhood in Queens. We eat calamari and potatoes with lemon at our favorite restaurant, sitting outside when the weather's warm, and then shop for spinach pie and *tzatziki* at the little deli down the block. Three hours in Athens—that's long enough, and far enough, for me.

Done

KISS A TOTAL STRANGER

As far as I'm concerned, the most stirring love scenes center on kissing. Long and deep or sweet and tender—it doesn't matter. When his hands go up to cup her face, it's all over. In fact, if the kissing's good, I don't need to see the sex.

If I ever had an affair, it would be a really short one—somewhere between five seconds and ten minutes. It would begin and end with kissing, and it would be with a total stranger. No commitments (I have a mate; I sure don't want another), not much talking, no real consequences. I'd get my kicks the way Katherine, an acquaintance of mine, did: in a sexy, spur-of-the-moment act of daring.

Katherine is forty-four and single, so there's really nothing stopping her from kissing strangers. (Since I'd like to hang on to my marriage, I'd have to get special dispensation from my husband to grab another man.) Katherine wasn't even dating anyone when she went to a friend's wedding and kissed not one, but three, total strangers in a single night.

I love this story.

The bride and groom were funky people, so Katherine had no qualms about wearing a '60s-era vintage dress, which she describes as "Donna Reed on acid," to the wedding. It was a beautiful spring day, and the dress certainly fit the mood. After the ceremony, which was held in a nineteenth-century mansion, there was a champagne toast. After the toast, the guests walked around the corner to the reception, where there were cocktails. After the cocktails, everybody was feeling flirty—especially Katherine.

Kiss number one came early. Katherine was talking with a cute guy in his mid-twenties. She asked him if he wanted to go outside for a cigarette. They were out there smoking and talking and laughing when she asked, "When are you going to kiss me?" After a second he said something like "Uh, okay," and they made out for a little while. (How long has it been since you used *that* term?)

Later, Katherine was dancing with an even younger man. He said, "You kissed that guy over there. Why'd you kiss him?" She said, "I don't know . . . 'cause I wanted to. Why, do you want me to kiss you, too?" And he said, "Okay, sure—what the hell." (They ended up dating for a few weeks after the wedding. Katherine goes out with young men fairly often, God love her.)

Kiss number three came at the end of the evening, as a group of friends was leaving. One of the men, who was in his early forties, wasn't exactly a party animal, but as they were saying their goodbyes, Katherine planted one on him, too. Unlike the young men, he was fairly flummoxed.

What triumph!

"It was definitely my night," Katherine says. "I caught flack for it for a couple of weeks, but I wasn't too worried about what my friends would think. The best part was that I just didn't care who saw, or what the guy thought of me. I just wanted to say I could do it."

60. KISS A TOTAL STRANGER

BIKE ACROSS AMERICA

I t's hard to be a happy wanderer—or any other kind—when you're an adult. You've got responsibilities to fulfill and people counting on you. You can't just drop everything to backpack through Europe or bike across America. At least, that's what you tell yourself when you've given up dreaming about it.

Exploring new territory is enlightening. It keeps you young and gives you something to talk about at boring parties. It's also very empowering to head off into the unknown and come back calling it your own. Why do you just assume that if you didn't do it in your twenties, you'll never do it?

By saving and planning carefully, you might be able to take a leave of absence from work. Or if you're planning to switch jobs or careers anyway, you could quit first and take a break before looking for work. Even if you can't swing the time off, you don't have to pull up stakes and spend the rest of your life at home. There's no minimum time requirement for exploration, so instead of biking across America, you can bike across your state.

If time and money aren't a problem, you may have to come up with other excuses, such as:

- You're too old.
- You're out of shape.
- You can't leave your house empty for that long.
- It's too much for the kids.

- The world is more dangerous than it used to be.

And here are some responses to your concerns:

- Get over it.
- So exercise.
- Find someone responsible to house-sit.
- Go slowly, stop a lot, and stay at motels with a pool.
- Tell that to the legions of twentysomethings who have the time of their lives traveling and never have a single encounter with the bogeyman.

Either you want to go, or you don't.

Peg Krygowski had always wanted to bike across the country. She and her husband, Frank, had been avid cyclists for years, but by the time she was in her mid-fifties, they both had knee problems. Krygowski, who's sixty-three now, figured that this was one adventure she and Frank would never have—but then their daughter graduated from college and said she wanted to bike across America with them before she settled down.

The timing couldn't have been better. Frank, a college professor, was off for the summer, and Krygowski was working as a physical therapist on an as-needed basis. Frank jumped on the idea, knees or no knees. Krygowski held back, saying she would drive along with them as backup. Not an option. "They were insistent," she says of her husband and daughter. "They didn't want any backup. It was 'Either you do this or you don't come.'"

So the three of them started in Delaware, dipping their back tires in the Atlantic. After riding six to seven hours a day for three and a half months, they finished in Oregon, dipping their front tires in the Pacific. For Krygowski, it was a lesson in "never say never." "If it's something you really want to do, you're going to be able to do it," she says. "Everyone just puts limitations on themselves."

Oh, and the knees held up just fine.

Done

PLAY IN THE SNOW

Close your eyes. Imagine a beautiful, peaceful snowfall. Picture yourself curled up on the couch with a cup of hot tea—chai, maybe, or Earl Grey—looking out the window at the white landscape around you. It's so pretty, so bright. You could bundle up nice and warm, and head out into the soft snow. You absolutely could.

But if you did, you'd get a chunk of snow in your boot. While digging it out, you'd get another one up your sleeve. Picture that. Your cheeks would sting and your nose would start running. God, how do kids do it? They stay out there for hours, soaking wet and freezing. They have icicles forming in their hair, but they don't care.

Neither did you when you were young. So when did you become so delicate? Imagine bundling up and actually playing in the snow, instead of just shoveling it. You could build a fort or make a snowman or chuck some snowballs. You could feel young and invigorated, instead of poopy and old. If only you could stand a little discomfort, you might have a lot of fun.

If you skied, you'd know this already. Skiers embrace the snow. Snow bunnies like Lynne Macco look *forward* to it. Here's why:

In 1998, when Macco was forty and divorced, she took her thirteen-year-old daughter on a two-day camping trip in Canada, in the woods just north of Quebec province. They stayed in a cabin on a gorgeous lake in a totally isolated area. It was the dead of winter, and the two of them were there to go dogsledding.

That first night in the cabin, they could hear the dogs outside. "You get a real sense of how close to wolves they are when you're out there camping with them. In the dark at night, they just start howling. It was just fantastic."

The first morning, they left the cabin with two guides, two other guests, four sleds, and twenty-four dogs. The group sledded for six hours, breaking for a cup of hot chocolate, until they reached the second night's accommodation: a hut in the woods. Macco's daughter stood on the back of the sled and drove it almost the entire way, yelling commands at the dogs.

"There is a brake, but all the steering is by the dogs staying on the path," says Macco. "I tried driving, but I took a turn really fast and flipped my daughter out of the sled, and she decided I wasn't qualified. It was very empowering for her."

Some time after that trip, Macco married a man who shares her sense of adventure—and her love of snow. In the winter of 2007, they took a hut-to-hut cross-country ski trip in the Colorado Rockies, visiting ten mountain huts that were built during World War II to house Army ski troopers training to scale Italy's Apennine Mountains to fight the Germans.

The winter before that, Macco and her husband skied in Yellowstone. "It's a fantastic time to go," she says. "You can't drive in. There's a seven- to twelve-foot base of snow, so rangers pick you up in snowcats, which are vehicles from World War II. They're like primitive snowmobiles. It was wonderful. There were only eighty people total; we felt like we had the park to ourselves."

RIDE IN A
FIRE TRUCK

There's a reason they don't make hunky-orthodontist calendars. While I'm sure that profession is not without its share of beefcakes, it can't come close to the number of gorgeous men living and working in firehouses. If you want to send your temperature through the roof, just hop on a fire truck one day and go for a spin.

In 2003, my friend Farida and I were in SoHo, in lower Manhattan, enjoying a girls' day out. The itinerary (as you might imagine if you've ever been there) included shopping, drinking, eating, and more shopping. Farida was about to move back to Toronto, and this was our last hurrah.

After two hours of drooling over shoes, bags, and designer clothes, we were starving for lunch. We decided to eat at Blue Ribbon Sushi, a neighborhood institution, but I couldn't remember what block it was on. We walked up and down a couple of SoHo's smaller streets and couldn't find the restaurant. Just as we were about to give up, a fire truck pulled in front of the meat market just behind us.

I don't know what possessed me, but I walked up to the truck's open window and asked the man behind the wheel if he knew where the sushi place was. And what a man he was: sandy hair, broad shoulders, big smile. He started giving me directions, but then stopped and said, "Hop in. We'll give you a ride."

Hop in . . . with the firefighters. Could this be real?

I went around to the other side of the truck and climbed in, assisted by another uniformed hunka hunka burning love. I sat in a tiny jump seat opposite him, our knees touching. Farida climbed in from the curb, but there was no jump seat on that side, so she had to sit on a firefighter's lap. Unbelievable.

The restaurant was just around the corner, but our ride was nice and slow. I had never been in the presence of so much male beauty—and unless I'm invited to the Academy Awards or a strip poker game with George Clooney and Brad Pitt, I won't ever be again. I wasn't in any rush to get to lunch.

Now, if a call had come in from the station house at that point, the thrill factor would have risen exponentially. Imagine barreling through the streets of New York in a seventy-five-thousand-pound emergency vehicle—horn blaring, siren screaming, lights flashing. As powerful and strong as our firefighters were, their truck was truly awesome.

Even if no hunky men had been onboard—and we had somehow landed on the only all-female fire truck in the city—the experience of speeding to an emergency would have set our hearts racing. For sheer drama, you can't beat it, unless you go for a ride in an ambulance (see "Join an Ambulance Crew" on page 30).

But we weren't on an all-woman truck—and we weren't on an emergency run. So we had to settle for the cheap thrill of riding around the block with some really handsome men in uniform. Boo-hoo.

63. RIDE IN A FIRE TRUCK

WATCH PORN

You'll be happy to know that a lot of people are thinking about your sexual enjoyment. For more than two decades, in fact, the adult-film industry has been trying to reel you in with X-rated movies made especially with women's sensibilities in mind—gal-style porn. So if you're not morally or politically opposed to adult entertainment, what's keeping you away? Are you just not interested . . . or are you afraid that you might be?

It's easy enough to find out. Every sex product imaginable is available online (see "Buy Yourself a Sex Toy" on page 74), and with movies, you don't even have to wait for the delivery truck to pull up. You can choose from hundreds of titles—including women's favorites like *Chemistry* and *Stunt Girl*—and download them onto your computer. Some might make your hair stand on end. But that doesn't mean the woman next to you won't love them.

Figuring out what women find arousing is not an exact science, but makers of adult films think they have a general idea of what you want to see:

- Better-looking men
- More communication between couples
- More loving interactions
- Less-contrived sex
- Better style sense (classy lingerie, great shoes, cool hairstyles, and so on)
- Women with more natural-looking bodies

Sounds good ... if you want to watch chick porn. But maybe you're more curious about what men find exciting; if so, you'll have a much larger inventory to choose from. But beware—you may not like what you find.

Katherine, who's forty-four and single, had a boyfriend who loved porn so much that he downloaded it every day. While he was at work one day, Katherine decided to see what she'd been missing. "There were a lot of girls who were not of age," she says. "It was horrible and illegal and disturbing. There were also a lot of icky body parts colliding. Bad makeup. Bad dialogue."

Finally, though, she found something she thought was erotic—a movie featuring burlesque superstar Dita Von Teese, who's famous for splashing around in a giant martini glass onstage, wearing pasties and a thong. Von Teese, who is stunning, is all about 1940s-style glamour—she's got great shoes, classy lingerie, and fabulous pin-up hair—and her sophisticated style may have been what Katherine found so sensual. "It was very stylized, very coy," she says. "There was a performing aspect to it."

Watching her boyfriend's movies proved enlightening for Katherine, and she's glad she snuck a peek. "I was able to learn about him through porn," she says. "It's part of his sexuality. I think the fact that he was very open about his passion for porn was actually very liberating. When I told him I had watched, he said, 'Really? Well, tell me what you think of it.'

"I also lost my sense of superiority about porn," she adds. "I shouldn't talk about it if I've never seen it."

Katherine might even consider watching some adult films on her own now, if they have high production value: "It might be fun to order some that get good ratings from women. It would be great if it was great."

SKINNY-DIP

You can do many pleasurable things when you're naked. You can take a hot, relaxing shower. You can have great sex. And you can immerse yourself in a body of water and feel as free and natural as a baby in a bathtub.

Skinny-dipping is one of the simplest, most sensuous experiences you can have, provided you don't have a problem with nudity. More often than not, you're dipping with others. Swimming nude liberates the mind and the body (see the related "Go Topless" on page 170), and it can be as naughty or as nice as you like. I recommend that you watch the following movies to get a sense of your preference:

SWEET: *ON GOLDEN POND*
Katharine Hepburn and Jane Fonda, as mother and daughter, bond in the buff during a night swim. They laugh and talk with an openness I hope to have with my daughter twenty years from now, with or without our clothes on.

SEXY: *A WALK ON THE MOON*
Diane Lane, a frustrated young housewife, has an affair in the summer of 1969 with Viggo Mortensen, the hippie "Blouse Man" who sells clothes out of his truck. Two gorgeous naked people making out under a waterfall—works for me.

STEAMY: *LAUREL CANYON*

Frances McDormand is a middle-aged record producer in L.A. who lives like it's still 1975. In a thoroughly decadent and erotic scene, she frolics in her backyard pool with her young rock-musician lover *and* her son's uptight fiancée.

Chances are, you're not going to be skinny-dipping with young rock stars. More likely, you'll shed your clothes and get wet with a bunch of women, whether they're friends, family, or—in the cases of Kim Merkin and my friend Lisa—total strangers.

For Lisa, who's forty-four, skinny-dipping was a way to resolve body-image issues. When she turned forty, she went to the Kripalu Center for Yoga and Health in western Massachusetts and ended up in the Kripalu Baths with twenty women she didn't know. The experience was a real test for Lisa, who had always been afraid of being seen naked.

"The lights were dimmed and it was very cavelike," she says. "You can feel the water on the more sensitive parts of your body; your breasts get to feel the water. It's very different than the bathtub. It's exciting. Daring. Adventurous. I'm walking where I don't usually go, outside the comfort zone."

For Merkin, who's also forty-four, skinny-dipping *was* the comfort zone. She has no problem with nudity, and when she went to Club Med Turks and Caicos for her friend's fiftieth birthday celebration (see "Plan a Girls' Vacation" on page 152), she skinny-dipped in the Caribbean Sea every night with one of the other birthday guests—a woman she'd never met before. After dancing for hours, they'd walk down to the water, drop their sweaty clothes, and dive right in.

"It was like rolling around in a luxurious set of sheets," Merkin says. "It's a salty body of water, so you're buoyant. We rolled and splashed around in the water, and felt uninhibited because we were naked. The sensation of the water on your body . . . it's so joyous. It's freeing."

BREAK A LONG-HELD TRADITION

If you have children, chances are you have myriad traditions that you work slavishly to uphold: holiday meals, birthday funfests, Memorial Day/July Fourth/Labor Day barbeques, and so on. You think (and rightly so) that happy rituals and continuity are meaningful to kids and that, if you create good memories, they'll do the same when it's their turn.

The thing about traditions, however, is that you can break them without consequence, as long as you replace them with something equally memorable. The particulars don't matter; if you switch from turkey to tofu loaf, the children may not like it, but they'll accept it as the new custom. They might even get into molding and dressing the thing, and make that *their* ritual contribution. Your mother may not be so flexible, but that's a different story (or perhaps it's the whole point).

For a few years, we took our kids to New York City during Christmas break to see a Broadway show and spend the night in a hotel—even though we live only twelve miles away. Playing tourists was part of the fun. We did this only three or four times, but when someone asked our daughter to describe her favorite family tradition, that's what she picked—as if we'd done it her whole life. Forget the annual holiday festivities and beach vacation; this new event took the prize.

A friend of mine, Kathleen, broke ranks over St. Patrick's Day when her children were young. It had always been a big holiday in her family, involving many rituals: Everyone dressed in green; everyone ate corned beef, potatoes, and cabbage; and many of them drank way too much. Kathleen, who's forty-seven, kept up the tradition until she realized one day that the holiday had no meaning to her—other than reminding her of unpleasantness. After that, she stopped celebrating entirely.

"My husband was relieved," she says. "If any of my family was involved, it would move from one or two Guinnesses to inebriation."

Her children didn't miss the festivities either, because Kathleen has always reinvented family customs anyway. "I set out to do things different than what I grew up with," she says. For example, she started a winter solstice celebration, which she likes better than Christmas because it involves no gift giving. Instead, she invites friends over to light candles, decorate the tree, and eat a special meal. Birthdays were always a big deal when Kathleen was growing up, and she makes them important in her home, too—but the focus is more on the meal, the cake, and the candles than on the presents.

In 2007, Kathleen introduced a holiday project that's destined to become a new tradition. She pulled out all of the family photos and put them on a side table, along with a photo album, glue, and scraps of art paper she had collected over the years. When relatives felt inspired, they could choose a photo, write the story of what they remembered about that moment, and create a brand-new page of family memories.

JOIN THE PEACE CORPS

Had they chosen differently, Nola Nackerud and her husband would have spent 1973–1975 in rural Venezuela with the Peace Corps. They applied to the program as newlyweds, but by the time they were accepted, Nackerud's husband had gotten a great job in Montana, so they declined. Another time, they told each other.

It took nearly thirty years, but another time finally came for Nackerud in 2001, after her husband walked out on her. She was fifty.

"I never forgot about the Peace Corps," she says in an email from Nicaragua, where she completed six years of service, from 2001 to 2007. "Whenever I would meet a Peace Corps volunteer, I thought it was such a good and neat thing to do.

"When my husband left me, I was devastated. People were asking, 'What are you going to do now?' I decided that instead of being sad and wallowing in my sorrow, I should turn it around and help others. Well, that old desire for the Peace Corps was reawakened in me, and I decided to try and apply. When the letter came and it was 'Yes, you are going to Nicaragua,' I was overjoyed and very proud.

"When I met my group that I was going to Nicaragua with, I felt so nervous. I was one of the oldest ones, and I was thinking, *Two years is so long*, and I was a bit teary eyed. But it got better each day from there."

During her service, Nackerud worked at four schools, three of them in very rural areas. To get to one, she had to cross a river on foot; when the river was high, she'd borrow a horse. Over the years, Nackerud helped to build a small library for the schools, along with a garden and a nursery. Parents and community members sold vegetables from the garden to help finance the library and built a small park with trees from the nursery. Nackerud also worked on projects ranging from reforestation to trash management to organic composting.

DOING TIME

The Peace Corps requires a twenty-seven-month commitment, so you'd better not get homesick. The first three months are for intensive language and technical training, followed by two years in your designated country. You can return home during your vacation time, but the Peace Corps encourages you to stay and travel around your country or region of service.

But Nackerud's greatest passion has been her work with deaf children. After learning sign language, she began teaching it to hearing students. She organized exchanges between deaf and hearing students, and created programs to educate the community about deafness. At the end of Nackerud's service, she was invited to come back and continue her work for minimal pay.

"I went home in September 2007 to my sister's house," Nackerud writes. "I had my things in storage at my nephew's, so I decided to sell thirty years of my life, of my married life, and I used that money to fly back here. I earn enough to pay my rent and eat—and not much more— but right now, I treasure every day that I am here.

"I truly believe that if I had stayed in the States after my divorce, I would have been very depressed and just not cared about living anymore. The Peace Corps gave me life again, and the people of Nicaragua nursed me back to living a meaningful and rich life. I learned that material things were a burden, and what was important was helping, loving, and being positive, and to care—and care deeply—about people."

PLAN A GIRLS' VACATION

As soon as my sister and I hit thirty-nine (no, we're not twins; I was adopted), we declared our intentions for our fortieth birthdays. We were going away—somewhere really great— just the two of us. No husbands. No kids. We stated it as fact, and nobody questioned it.

The criteria for picking the destination were simple. It had to be a place our husbands would never want to visit, and, more important, a place that would make our female friends and colleagues jealous. A week in Florida wouldn't cut it. We thought briefly about Hawaii, but it was too . . . American. We needed an exotic locale. So we went to Capri, the small island off the coast of Italy that is the playground of the rich and famous. Mariah Carey has a villa there; so does Giorgio Armani. It's also where Rod Stewart honeymooned and Liz Hurley reportedly shopped for wedding dresses.

Here's what we did that our husbands would never have done (not happily, at least): We window-shopped. In addition to featuring many smaller and more modest shops, the streets of Capri are lined with Gucci, Armani, Ferragamo, and Pucci stores—not quite our style but fun to look at. We checked out jewelry, shoes, and handbags. We ate lunch and dinner at lovely restaurants with spectacular views and had cocktails every afternoon in the piazza. We went to the spa and lay out at the pool. We did make it to the Blue Grotto, but we were so happy being slugs that we blew off our planned excursion to Pompeii.

And that was just the first half of our trip. After four days on the island, we spent another four in Rome, doing more shopping, drinking, and eating. We also managed to catch some of the sights: the Vatican, the Forum, the Colosseum, the Pantheon, and the Borghese Gardens. Best of all, we had ten uninterrupted days to hang out and have fun together. It was the perfect chick trip.

My friend Jackie's fortieth-birthday getaway with the girls wasn't so perfect. In their case (as in my sister's and mine), it all came down to location, location, location. The four women had trouble agreeing on a destination. Two wanted to go to a spa; the other two, including Jackie, wanted to do Vegas. So they compromised: two nights at a resort just outside of town, and two nights on the strip—R&R first, partying second. But the four forty-year-olds weren't the party animals they had once been.

"We were just too tired to stay out late," says Jackie, who's now forty-two. "We were back at the rooms and asleep by midnight. The resort was more fun. We could sit in the Jacuzzi, walk around in our white robes, and lounge around on outdoor chairs. We could catch up more. I was wrong; we had a vision of ourselves . . . and it was totally the wrong vision."

For Barbara Critchlow, choosing a destination was a no-brainer. To celebrate her fiftieth, she invited more than twenty female friends from all over the United States to go to the Club Med resort on Turks and Caicos in the Caribbean. She'd make all the arrangements; they'd just have to pay their way and show up. Club Med's all-inclusive aspect made it easy: Everyone knew the cost up front, and nobody had to make any decisions the entire week.

In the end, five women went—and they had a blast. "We started drinking cocktails on the plane first thing in the morning; we were disappointed that the airport bar wasn't open," says Critchlow. "By the time we landed, we were happy."

LEARN
SURVIVAL SKILLS

R
emember Euell Gibbons, the outdoorsman and natural-foods guru who claimed that Grape-Nuts cereal tasted like wild hickory nuts? Maybe it was his cheesy 1970s commercials that piqued your interest in wilderness survival, or the 2004 *Survivorman* episode, where Les has to survive a week in the Boreal Forest of Northern Canada, armed only with a match, a multitool, beef jerky, and some cashews.

Neither one did it for me. I don't participate in any activity that involves knives, tents, or walking sticks. But I can certainly understand the appeal of living in nature and being self-reliant—especially after talking to Sherry Pinkus. An avid backpacker, she's downed her share of dehydrated dinners.

"It's a perspective-gaining experience," says Pinkus, who's fifty-four. "Survival stuff is taken care of for us all the time. It's redefining to have that be the focus for a change."

Pinkus has never taken a survival-skills class, although they're widely available; instead, she's taught herself by reading, asking, and doing. "You learn how to negotiate your whereabouts using a map and compass," she says. "You learn how to pack so you can survive on your own. You learn how to conduct yourself in the outdoors to avoid trouble. For instance, you never cook in the clothing that you are sleeping in."

Pinkus made a plan to backpack through Mount Rainier National Park in Washington with her sixteen-year-old daughter in the summer of 2008. She obtained a cross-country permit, which meant they'd be off the trails, in the wilderness, just the two of them. They'd be in three different terrains—lowlands, subalpine, and alpine—hiking through woods and meadows and on glacial rock.

For this trip, Pinkus learned a new survival skill: how to deal with bears. The trees in the park aren't high enough to stash food, so, for the first time, she needed to use a bear canister for storage. "Unless that bear is carrying a Phillips-head screwdriver," she says, "he can't open it up.

"You have to know what's in the area and be proactive about that. With bears, for example, you never bring anything with a scent into the tent with you: no shampoo, deodorant, soap. You wash up with biodegradable soap that is unscented."

Pinkus's survival kit is fairly simple. Item number one is a multitool knife with pliers. To purify water, she brings special tablets and a filter. (Boiling water uses too much fuel.) Instead of matches and fire starter, she carries a miniscule propane-fueled stove (better for the environment). Rations include instant oatmeal, dry cheeses, salami and pepperoni, dried fruits, and dehydrated dinners.

"It's one of the best parts of the trip for me, that food is not an issue," Pinkus says. "It sustains me, there's enough to feed me, but I don't think about menus. It's how I relax, how I let go of all the other stuff."

WHEN YOU SEE A BEAR AND IT SEES YOU

You actually want bears to know that you're around; that lessens the chance that you'll have a sudden encounter, which they really don't like. Shout, sing, or make other loud noises as you hike. If a bear sees you but hasn't acted aggressively, slowly back away. Don't run; that may elicit an attack from an otherwise nonaggressive animal. Plus, it'll beat you. You wouldn't know it to look at them, but bears can run at speeds of thirty-plus miles per hour.

PAINT YOUR HOUSE A WILD COLOR

I wasn't a wild child, and so far I'm not a wild woman. I have some regrets about that, but the truth is, I just don't have it in me. I'm too big a sissy to break all the rules, so I've had to find other ways to set myself apart. In high school I would never have dreamed of sneaking out to go bar-hopping, but I was the first kid with a pair of L.L.Bean Duck Boots. I thought they were really cool . . . in an ugly sort of way. And while I didn't wear them to be noticed, I liked that they were different. They were me.

I'd still like to stand out, to wear my individuality on my feet (or car or house), but I've gotten more conservative in my old age. Case in point: The last time we painted our house, in 2002, I wanted to break out and try a bold color, something deeper and darker than the medium gray it had been since we'd bought it. I enlisted the help of a friend whose house is a terrific shade of forest green and who was thinking of going into the color-consulting business.

After looking at the house and talking to me, she came up with a color grouping that looked great but was much bolder than I would have picked. The house color would be a leafy green and the trim a beige with a yellow cast. Green and yellowy beige. My roof tiles are industrial gray with specks of white and black; what if it clashed? I went to the hardware store and started looking at chips myself—and ended up with the most boring dark blue with seafoam green trim.

I hate it. And I hate that I backed out of the vivid scheme my friend selected. Maybe I've become as drab as my house. Maybe *that* is me. But it certainly isn't Donna Dickert, who's become more daring in her old age, not less.

In 2006, when she was fifty-three, Dickert moved back to her house in New Jersey after living for four years in London. One of the first things she did was repaint it a wild color. When she and her husband had first bought the house it was dark gray, and she'd immediately covered it with pale turquoise. Now, even that looked dull.

The row houses in her London neighborhood were bright. One of her favorite blocks was a virtual color wheel, with shades of lavender, blue, yellow, and pink. "I liked seeing it when it was raining and dreary," she says. "Every day when I walked the kids to school, it made me happy to walk by that block."

So she chose new colors for her three-bedroom, side-hall Colonial that had a similar feel: Benjamin Moore's Honolulu Blue for the house, Utah Sky for the shutters, and Softened Violet for the door. The other houses on her block were white and beige.

When the primer coat went up, even Dickert was shocked. "The neighbors were saying, 'Oh my god, it's so bright.' It was like being in elementary school." But when it was done, Dickert and her family loved it. Who cared what anyone else thought?

"I feel really happy," she says. "When we drive down the street, we say we have the nicest house, even though it's the smallest house. It feels very cheerful. The kids come in and say, 'I love the house.' It's the best thing."

TRY HIGH-STAKES GAMBLING

Being reckless with money isn't generally a laudable trait. You don't hear people say, "Good for you, you pissed it all away!" or, "Wish I'd thought of flushing mine down the toilet." But if once in a blue moon—or once in your life—you decide to gamble big, you'll be so flush with excitement, you won't care what other people say.

It's positively wicked to throw away money, which is what usually happens when you gamble. You can try to justify it by setting a dollar limit for yourself—$50, $75, $100—and saying you'd spend that on a night out anyway. But that's not gambling; that's trading your sushi boat and your comedy-club ticket for a few chips and a slice of pepperoni pizza.

The fun comes from saying, "Screw the odds, I'm going for broke." It takes chutzpah to put real money on the table and confidence to feel that you can afford to lose it. The actual dollar amount is irrelevant—it can be $200 or $2,000—as long as it seems like a lot to you. (For more on the concept of relative values, see "Buy Something Outrageously Expensive" on page 132.) However much you bet, you have to appreciate the difference between playing it safe and taking big risks.

Imagine being at the horse track. You pick up the racing form, check the odds, and decide to bet on Fast Forward, the odds-on favorite, to win. When you get to the betting window, you pull out a twenty and place your bet. Back at your seat, you cheer as Fast Forward rounds the bend and crosses the finish line first. You've just doubled your money.

Now imagine the same scenario, except when you go to the window, you put down $200. Ten times the loss; ten times the gain. Back at your seat, you're keyed up. You could lose $200 in a matter of minutes. Or you could walk home $200 richer. At the sound of the starting gun, you leap up and scream at the top of your lungs. Go, Fast Forward, go!

Scenario two is much funner. And unless you're a habitual high-stakes gambler (which is a whole other story), isn't that the point?

Lisa Lee works weekends as a croupier at a card club in California, where most customers are compulsive gamblers hoping to make money to pay their bills. Not a happy bunch. But for a time, she had two customers who really stood out.

"They were women in their mid-fifties, and they were nurses," says Lee, who's fifty-one. "There's a nursing shortage in the Bay Area, and they were here for six or eight weeks to work. The two of them were delightful. We were all laughing; they were a lot of fun, and they tipped me really well. One of them lost all her money—a couple of hundred dollars. But they were out having a great time; they were just busting out."

I doubt they would have had even half the fun if they'd limited themselves to $50.

MONEY FOR (NEXT TO) NOTHING

As great as it is to gamble big and win big, it's even better to gamble spare change and win a five-figure sum. In July 2006, a woman in Michigan placed a ten-cent superfecta bet on a horse race being simulcast from California, and she won $21,584.

PLAY
ICE HOCKEY

On February 13, 1976, at the Olympic Winter Games in Innsbruck, Austria, Dorothy Hamill won the gold medal in women's figure skating. That same year Bobby Clarke, of the Philadelphia Flyers, won the Hart Memorial Trophy for the NHL's Most Valuable Player. Both were admirable athletes, but I can tell you this: It wasn't Clarke who inspired my sister and me to run out and take skating lessons at age fourteen, or who motivated ten billion girls (including me) to get a wedge haircut. I didn't know Clarke existed, and I wouldn't have cared much if I had.

If I'd grown up in a hockey family, maybe Clarke's victory would have sent me running to the rink (not that there was a girls' hockey class for me to take). But that wasn't the case. Annie Scales, on the other hand, had a mother who adored Bobby Orr, and was so into hockey that she coached her son's team. Scales skated until she was eleven, when her mother died, and then she wouldn't skate again until her own son asked her to try. She was almost forty—the same age her mother was when she died.

Scales had been watching her son practice and play from the time he was four. "I used to hate going to the rink," she says. "It was so cold, and I didn't understand the game." But in 2007, when he was ten, her son told her about a rumor circulating among his teammates: Some of the mothers were forming a team of their own. Would she join?

How could she not at least give it a shot? Scales signed on, bought some used gear, and started training.

The Mother Puckers, as they called themselves, had hired the coach of the thirteen-year-old-girls' team. They began with nine weeks of basic skills, followed by three weeks of scrimmages against each other. Some of them had never skated before; others had skated in high school. Scales was nervous at first, but that didn't last long. "Once I got out there, I saw that there were people on the team who were at different levels, and the nervousness went away," she says.

After twelve weeks of training, the team played its first scrimmage against a rival team: the thirteen-year-old boys. And then, on a Friday night, the women played their first game—against the thirteen-year-old girls. The Puckers lost, 5 to 2, but it was the beginning of their competitive career, and they started playing other women's teams.

Women's recreational hockey leagues have been springing up around the country, and the Puckers' first official season was in the fall of 2007. When the season ended, they went right back to skills training and maintained their competitive edge by playing against their kids' teams. The kids usually won.

"Whenever we can get ice time, we play," says Scales. "It's constant. We play once or twice a week for an hour."

The Mother Puckers' 2008 spring season was a much different experience. "It was more intense, more ferocious," says Scales. "We all got out there, we all knew how to skate, and we knew the game. I'm excited. It's fun; we have a good time. And my son loves watching. He's very proud of me."

That's the real benefit of playing hockey for Scales: It keeps her close to her son. And, unexpectedly, it's brought her closer to her mother.

THROW AN ALL-GIRLS PARTY

When my friend Peg turned forty, she threw herself a party. She had forty-two guests—all women—of various ages and from different parts of her life. There were friends from exercise class, from the neighborhood, from the Little League sidelines. There were work friends and old friends and the friends you make along the way who become as essential to your daily life as your morning cup of coffee. And there were family members: mother, sister, mother-in-law, and a few of *their* oldest friends.

The party started at an exercise studio, where Peg's regular instructor held a special class. All the guests were wearing sweats and no makeup and stayed that way for the rest of the night. Back at the house, eighty experienced hands helped set out the spread that Peg had prepared herself. Friends had brought fruit platters and salads and pitchers of cocktails. Peg's living room buzzed with dozens of women who were comfortable, chatty, and really happy to be there.

As an icebreaker (not that she needed one), Peg, who's now forty-four, taped a long strip of brown butcher paper across the wall and asked her guests to write a secret about themselves in marker, without any names attached. (Mine? Driving topless from Cape Cod to New Jersey one night when I was in my early twenties and on a girls' road trip.) Throughout the party, one of the guests walked around taking Polaroid pictures, and each woman had to tape her photo to the wall next to her secret.

It was one of the best parties I've ever been to. Peg, too.

"I knew if there were no men and you got everyone down to basics, there would be no pretense," she says. "Very little alcohol was drunk, because no one needed to loosen up. I didn't want to be running around at my fortieth birthday, checking to see if everyone is okay. I just wanted to have a party and not be an ambassador."

Kim Merkin, who's also forty-four, started having slumber parties (she calls them "slumbos") with her girlfriends when they were all in their late twenties. But once some of the women had children, the parties petered out. In her forties, Merkin revived them, adding a new crop of participants she'd met through a networking group that she started as a way to help women connect. (East Bay United Girls now numbers seventy-five members.)

"My forties have been all about creating connections," says Merkin. "I had a good foundation from my twenties and thirties."

The slumbos often have a theme; one time it was "tell a burn-in-hell story" about something naughty the guests had done. One woman in her fifties had slept with a man only a few years older than her son. After they fooled around, the lover would watch cartoons.

"Outrageous things come out," says Merkin. "No topic is taboo. Sex comes up still, although the stories aren't as racy as they were. We drink some wine, but nobody gets gross drunk. It's an intimate space where you share very personal stories and have a good laugh. One time we stayed up until three in the morning; last time we only made it until midnight.

"For two of the parties I threw, I hired masseuses. I used to cook for everybody, but last time I hired a private chef, and that was so nice—decadent and frivolous. I'd much rather spend this time with the people I've invited than run around and worry about the dishes."

MAKE A
SEX TAPE

After our second child was born, I asked my husband how the experience compared with the birth of our first. Without hesitating, he said, "To be honest, the first time was amazing . . . and the second time was just plain gross." I'm very grateful that the mirror in the delivery room was facing the other way.

There are certain parts of me I'd rather not see, and certain activities I'd rather not watch. I'll speak for myself, though, because plenty of women revel in seeing their children being born, just as many enjoy watching themselves in the throes of passion. Clearly, they don't have the issues I do.

For the issueless woman, making a sex tape can be an enlightening and stimulating experience. Affirming, too—in the same way posing for boudoir photographs is. (See "Have Nude Pictures Taken" on page 80.) You have to have made some kind of peace with your body to put your cellulite on celluloid.

"It's not that you need to look perfect," says Jamye Waxman, a sex educator and adult-cinema director. "You need to be comfortable seeing your body and understand that you are a beautiful being. You're going to see yourself from a different perspective—the third-party perspective—and if you don't want to be there, that's the end of the story."

But what if you *sort of* want to be there? How can you get past your inhibitions and insecurities? For starters, you can pretend. Having sex for the camera is a performance, after all, and while you don't want to fake the whole thing, a little role playing may help put you in the mood for real. "Don't feel like you have to do acrobatic positions," says Waxman. "But if there's a little dialogue—'Ahh, that feels good'—and you're acting sexy, you may find that it's a true turn-on. Or give yourself a persona—that is, permission to not be yourself—if it helps you get there. The goal is to show you in a genuine state of sexual satisfaction."

For your first sex tape, Waxman suggests you record yourself in a solo performance. "You'll see yourself on camera. You can play with lighting and with different angles. You can shoot it wide and show your whole body, then shoot it again, showing just your face. Or you can shoot what you're doing. You can think about what parts of your body you want to see on camera."

And what parts you don't.

In real life, if you're self-conscious about the state of your belly, there's nothing you can do. But on film there is. You can wear a miniskirt and lift it up over your waist. You can also shoot above, below, or around it. A trick of the porn trade, according to Waxman, is arching your back, which is uncomfortable during actual sex but looks good on film because it lengthens your body.

"Sexuality is already ingrained in all of us," says Waxman. "We need to keep growing sexually, and making a sex tape might give you new ideas."

COVER YOUR ASS

If you're making a sex tape with a partner, create a written agreement about how you're going to treat the tape. Come up with rules about keeping it private—where you're going to store it, how you're going to label it—and about what happens to it should you part ways. The contract may not be legally binding, but at least you've tried to exercise some control over material that could be damaging in the wrong hands.

LEARN TO DRIVE

You may be a freethinker, freewheeler, or free spirit, but if you're stuck at home because you can't drive, you're pretty much a prisoner. This is America—*everyone* drives, every chance we get, even when it costs $80 to fill up the gas tank. If the bank is four blocks away, we'll jump in the car, rather than walk the distance (although in much of the country, you're lucky if the nearest bank is four miles away).

We're so stuck on our cars that we identify one another by them. Hybrids mean you're politically correct (or cost-conscious), minivans mean you're a parent (or a dry cleaner), and an $80,000 sports car means somebody's had a really good year. When cars and their drivers don't match, it upsets the world order. What if Farrah Fawcett drove the Partridge family bus and Shirley Jones had the Mustang Cobra? That's just wrong.

So where does that leave you, as a nondriver in America? Dependent on others, for sure. Limited in what you can do. And perpetually identified as the woman who can't drive. You don't have to take that.

Barring any medical issues, you can learn to drive—even now. Is it scary? Absolutely. But if you want your freedom, you'll have to get past your fear. For Julie Finch, not driving wasn't a big issue until she bought a cottage in Maine when she was fifty-eight. A native New Yorker, she had spent every summer of her childhood in Maine with her mother and grandmother, neither of whom could drive. They took taxis everywhere.

When Finch closed on her cottage, her broker drove her to the closing. Throughout that spring, as she renovated the cottage, she took taxis everywhere to pick out all the materials. One day when she was at a flooring company with her mother, she called a taxi to pick them up— and it took twenty minutes to arrive. "That was my saturation limit," says Finch. "That did it."

She returned to New York and gave herself a deadline: one month to get her driver's license. She took lessons five days a week and scheduled practice sessions in between. "I was terrified, but determined," Finch says. "Once I decide to do something, I follow through." That August in Maine, she was able to drive herself around—as long as she stayed on local roads. The highway was too scary.

Finch's moment of truth came when she went to Texas to see her new grandson. She flew into Midland and rented a car. "I was so nervous about getting on the highway, I passed all the entrances and stayed on the service road until it led me there," she says. "I kept saying to myself, *I'm doing this for my baby grandson. I can do this.*"

Finch had to do it on the way back to Midland, too, only this time, as she drove at the legal minimum speed, she got stuck behind a truck that was going even slower than she was.

"I had to make a choice: Pass the truck or miss the plane," she says. "So I passed the truck at seventy-five miles per hour and made my plane. I felt fantastic. I told all my friends that I managed to get on the highway and that I managed to pass a truck. I felt like I was more of a grownup for empowering myself."

Freedom will do that to you.

Done

LIE ABOUT SOMETHING

I hate surprise parties. If I smell one in the works, my stomach knots up and I'm a pain to be around—anxious, suspicious, and obnoxious to everyone I think is in on it. I feel vaguely sick until the last person has popped out from behind the couch and I've had at least two drinks.

As much as I dislike being deceived, however, I love deceiving others. You can sign me up anytime for the role of ruse-meister or hoax facilitator. I delight in weaving lies and waving them right under the guest of honor's nose. I was in seventh heaven planning my husband's surprise fortieth and being an accomplice in our friend Mitch's fiftieth.

But my best performance by far was at my sister's bridal shower. The setup was perfect because Judy and I were already planning to get together and cook a big family dinner, which meant that she'd set aside a day to be at my house. The plot unfolded from there: She and I would spend two days shopping and cooking for what she thought was a family gathering but would in fact be her shower. An hour before the family was due to arrive for dinner, the doorbell would ring and the guests would file in.

I steered our menu selection for the dinner so that it could be extended easily to feed a crowd. Judy and I chose to make beef tenderloin, which I figured could be sliced thinner and paired with a chicken dish for the buffet table. Instead of baking a cake, I suggested that we make mousse cups, which could join other sweets on the dessert table. My mother, my sister Lauren, and my sister-in-law Tracey were in charge of the additional menu items.

POPULAR THINGS TO LIE ABOUT

- Past relationships
- Marital status
- How you lost your virginity
- Number of previous marriages
- What you earn
- What you spent
- Wild things you've done
- Rock stars you've met
- Rock stars or movie stars you've slept with
- Where you were

I spent many hours on the phone with Judy, planning, creating shopping lists, and divvying up responsibilities—all for an event that wasn't real. The more detailed the conversations became, the deeper into deception I went. It was like living in alternate realities: I'd be talking about making basil mashed potatoes for twelve while I was thinking about whether I could somehow turn that into potato wedges for thirty. The lying became easier and easier . . . as if it were the truth.

We spent the day of the event cooking like crazy. When the doorbell rang, we were in the kitchen, working away, covered in ingredients. Judy came out into the hall and was shocked when she saw the guests; she turned around and went back into the kitchen for five minutes to compose herself. The shower came off perfectly, the food was great, and there was plenty of it.

Here's where I messed up, however: Judy was pretty mad. While she conceded that I'd done a brilliant job at pulling the wool over her eyes, she thought I was mean for making her cook for her own shower. I was. Being a good liar can backfire on you.

GO TOPLESS

I've never understood this: How did we, the women of the United States, get to be such prudes about our bodies? And why do we choose to stay that way? Even though cleavage is in, and a small group of middle-aged women insist on showing more than their sixteen-year-olds do, the vast majority of us cover up as if we live in a convent. It's like there's no middle ground between dressing like an old tart and Sister Batrille.

When it comes to nudity, we've got issues. At the gym, we undress with our backs to each other; at home, we lock the bathroom door when we shower. Meanwhile, in France, women are so comfortable with themselves that they go topless at the beach—even if they're packing a little too much camembert around their midsection. And they couldn't care less that their children and grandchildren are frolicking in the sand next to them.

Which way sounds like more fun to you—theirs or ours?

TOP(LESS) FIVE DESTINATIONS

- Anse du Gouverneur
  St. Barts, French West Indies
- Black's Beach
  San Diego, California
- Clifton Beach
  Cape Town, South Africa
- Copacabana Beach
  Rio de Janeiro, Brazil
- Illetes
  Formentera, Spain

Source: *Forbes* magazine, 2006

If you've ever gone topless, you know how great it feels. If not, just imagine having nothing binding, poking, or scratching you; nothing clinging or restricting your movement. Then imagine the warmth of the sun and a soft breeze on your skin. Or just ask your husband or boy-friend to describe it for you. He knows.

So does Lisa Solod. She went swimming topless in Spain in 2004 on a vacation with her two children, who were ten and fifteen. The kids were embarrassed at first, but they had lived in France when they were younger and traveled a fair amount, so they had seen topless and nude women before.

Solod, who was forty-eight at the time, was a bit uncomfortable too. She was very aware of her actions as she rolled down her bathing suit top—and it took her half an hour to get used to it and relax. But once she did, she loved it.

"There was a rock pool and a gorgeous, gorgeous beach," she says. "I was much more conscious of my skin than ever before. The water felt like silk on my body. It's very tactile . . . like being stroked. I have really big boobs, and it was so freeing."

Going topless was emotionally liberating, too. Without realizing it, Solod had been working her way up to this day, taking little steps to get comfortable with her middle-aged body. "For years I wore clothes that were too big for me, as many American women do," she says. "My old roommate visited me once—she was French—and she said, 'Why are you wearing that?'"

When Solod moved to France in 2001, she was struck by how the women dressed—they bought clothes that fit—so she totally changed her wardrobe. "I decided I was going to show my chest," she says. So the minute she got into that rock pool in Spain, she thought, *Being topless is absolutely brilliant. Why did I ever wear a bathing suit? What a stupid thing to wear.*

SCUBA DIVE

If you want to travel to worlds unknown (to you, at least), you can go in one of two directions: up or down. Unless you can shell out $200,000 to blast off with Richard Branson, scuba diving might be the call. For a few hundred dollars, you can don a mask and oxygen tank and dive 0.005 leagues, or thirty feet, under the sea to one of the most beautiful and tranquil places in the universe.

In tropical waters, it looks as if someone took an open bottle of fairy dust and tossed it overboard. The sun shines through, lighting an underwater landscape of hot-pink coral, bright purple fish, and shiny silver sea snakes. The Disney Princesses would feel right at home.

One nice thing about diving is that you can try it without making a huge commitment. Many resorts and dive centers offer guided recreational dives that require just three hours of instruction and cost as little as $65. If you find that you love the feel of wet neoprene stuck to your skin, you can then take a two-part course (part one in a pool; part two in open water) and become a certified diver.

This, too, is relatively cheap. For example, the course at Diver's Den in St. Mary's, Georgia, costs $269, while the one at the Scuba Schools Group in Seattle costs $369. Not a lot to pay to visit a world so far removed from yours that you might never want to come up—that's assuming, of course, that you have the guts to go down in the first place.

Diving requires physical and mental strength. You have to carry a ton of equipment—a wetsuit, a buoyancy-compensation device, a regulator, a console, and an air tank—without herniating yourself. You have to wear a mask and a mouthpiece without getting claustrophobic. You have to have faith that when you sit on the edge of the boat and topple backward into the sea, you'll be able to right yourself in the water. And, of course, you have to accept that the only things keeping you alive are a tank on your back and a rubber hose in your mouth.

Alice Falkenstein was fifty-four when she got up the nerve and took a course, with her teenage daughter, through the worldwide diving organization PADI. For years she had gone to Club Med and thought about taking its free scuba classes, but she was too scared. What if she wasn't a strong enough swimmer? What if she tried and couldn't do it?

Finally, she wasn't afraid to risk it—but her first open-water dive, in Jamaica, didn't go well. Falkenstein's tank pulled her into the ocean before she was ready, she had trouble clearing her goggles, and she was so nervous that she dropped her mouthpiece. But once she got down there, she was struck by how beautiful it was.

"Why didn't I try when I was younger?" says Falkenstein, now sixty-two. "I could have been doing it all this time."

TOP TEN BEST DIVES*

- Bonaire
- Curaçao
- Little Cayman, Cayman Islands
- Grand Cayman Islands
- Cozumel, Mexico
- Dominica
- Providenciales, Turks and Caicos
- Puerto Rico
- Grand Turk, Turks and Caicos
- Roatan, Bay Islands, Honduras

*This list was compiled based on the votes of *Scuba Diving* magazine's readers.

GET A
BRAZILIAN WAX

There comes a point when even the most risk-averse women get tired of being weenies. That's when they go to the hairdresser and tell her to take it all off or dye it magenta (see "Drastically Change Your Hairstyle" on page 48). But women who really want to bust loose will skip the hairdresser, go straight to the hair *waxer,* and tell her to take it all off.

Removing all your pubic hair with a Brazilian wax might be too scary or creepy for you to contemplate—and who can blame you? It *is* painful, and it does make you look like a ten-year-old. But if you dare to go bare, you're in for a real surprise—and not a bad one. Many women like the feeling of having soft, smooth skin around their privates and say that it heightens their sexual pleasure. Even if you're doing it for your partner, you may be the primary beneficiary.

The term "Brazilian wax" can be confusing. In some salons it means total hair removal around the vagina, with a little patch left in the front—usually in the shape of a soul patch, a triangle, or a rectangle known as a landing strip. (This is a good option for women who are uncomfortable with the idea of looking like a little girl.) In other salons, it means the full Monty—not a single pubic hair left. Anywhere.

Brazilian waxes are relatively new in the United States. The J Sisters salon in New York City, owned by seven Brazilian-born sisters, first started doing them in 1994. Today, you can get one just about anywhere. If you're passing through Ozark, Missouri, the Serenity Day Spa will do the honors for $75—$10 more than the J Sisters charge at their Manhattan-townhouse salon.

THINGS YOU CAN DO TO MINIMIZE THE DISCOMFORT AND PROMOTE HEALING

- Exfoliate any ingrown-hair bumps, making light circular motions with a washcloth, so they can heal before your waxing.
- Take Ibuprofen or some other anti-inflammatory pain medication a few hours before your waxing.
- Apply a topical numbing cream, approved for use in the vaginal area, an hour before your appointment.
- To avoid irritation, wear loose clothing (no tight jeans) made from a breathable material, such as cotton, to your appointment.

The process can be a bit brutal—and embarrassing. You start on your back (naked, of course), with your knees bent and your feet on the table. One at a time, you bring your knees to your chest so that your attendant can work her way down. If she needs better access, you may have to get up on the table on all fours. Other than that, it's like any other waxing procedure: Working in sections, the aesthetician applies a thin layer of warm wax to your skin, covers it with a cloth strip, and then rips off the strip, going against the grain of your hair.

And the pain . . . well, it hurts. As one acquaintance described it, "It feels like someone hit you in the privates with a frying pan."

USE FOOD AS FOREPLAY

In the history of cinema, a handful of scenes are as legendary as the movies they come from: the beach embrace in *From Here to Eternity,* the horse's head in *The Godfather,* and the jog up the museum steps in *Rocky.* And then there are memorable moments from thoroughly forgettable films, such as the ice cube scene in *9½ Weeks.*

In that 1986 erotic drama, Mickey Rourke empties half the contents of the refrigerator onto, and into, Kim Basinger, with whom he's having a sadomasochistic affair. On the kitchen floor, he teases and titillates her with olives, tomatoes (I think), Jell-O, champagne, milk, and, of course, strawberries. And in the bedroom, as she lies blindfolded on the bed, he caresses her with an ice cube—running it across her lips, down her chest, around her belly, and along the top of her panties. Who can forget that?

Not Christine Garofoli; she couldn't help but think of that scene when her boyfriend surprised her one night with strawberries and melted chocolate—in bed. They'd come back to his apartment after having dinner out, and he had it all set up: flowers on the floor leading to the bedroom, candles, and the special dessert course.

"That was such a cheesy movie; I was a little apprehensive about doing it," says Garofoli, who's forty. "He started drizzling the chocolate on my stomach and my chest. Then he took the strawberries and dipped them into the chocolate.

"It felt contrived—and in my mind, I was giggling. But once we started getting into it and were pressed up against each other, him licking it off of me and me licking it off of him, it was steamy. It felt really good; the physical sensation got me into the moment, instead of thinking of the moment.

"At one point the chocolate was too hot and we had to wait for it to cool off. So we made out, we giggled and cuddled, and we talked chocolate. The lovemaking was very intense and passionate. It was the thrill of doing something different. It was fun and naughty, and we definitely bonded over it. We had done something that was really cool.

"There was something about his planning this beforehand that was really special. He got the chocolate, he melted it.... That's any woman's dream. When we came back from dinner, I thought, *Ooooh, this is going to be an interesting evening.*"

Using food as foreplay was an exciting experience, but Garofoli hasn't repeated it. Maybe that's because it happened in another life—when she was in her twenties, before marriage and children. But she thinks about that drizzled chocolate at least once a year. Why hasn't she done it again? Good question. No good answer.

"Have I gotten too fuddy-duddy about making a mess of the sheets?" wonders Garofoli. "My husband would love to do something like this, but he's a little more nervous. I'd have to initiate it with him.

"We're going away for the weekend. Hmm . . . that's the perfect time to do it—in the hotel's bed. I think he would love it. He'd think it was hot."

START A CHARITY

In 2007, Melinda Gates's foundation gave away $2 billion to support projects around the world. Marianne Emerson's foundation donated $58,000 to two high school teachers in Minneapolis and to six other groups that help immigrants learn English. Gates's foundation has 520 employees; Emerson's has one employee, plus two volunteers who chipped in when she needed help. As for the amount of love and devotion behind each effort—there's no measure for that.

Emerson started the Ray Solem Foundation, named after her husband, six months after he died of a heart attack in 2006. It was his idea; in fact, he stipulated in his will that the bulk of his estate should be spent on this cause. Solem, who had worked for the United States Agency for International Development, had always admired immigrants. Later, as a commercial real estate broker, he worked with many Latinos and helped them develop business skills.

Solem and Emerson often talked about his wishes—and their own personal riches: good health, family, money, and careers that they loved. Emerson, who's sixty, knew she'd be carrying out his plan: He had named her executor of his estate, trustee of his trust, and president of his foundation. She just didn't expect to be doing it so soon.

"Other than giving money, I hadn't done anything to help others," she says. "Had Ray lived longer, I would have helped support him in his efforts."

It didn't take Emerson long to figure out how to launch the foundation. She bought a book on forming a nonprofit corporation and downloaded the necessary forms from the Internal Revenue Service's website. "Ray was a businessperson, so I knew how to incorporate a business," she says. "I soaked up some business knowledge from being around him. . . . I did his books."

Deciding how to appropriate the grant money proved harder. From a friend of a friend, Emerson got the idea to hold a contest among nonprofit organizations to determine the most creative approach to teaching English-language skills. She posted the criteria on her foundation's website and got the word out through the Council of Foundations. She received 425 applications.

Emerson set up a committee to judge them; it included her, Ray's cousin, and a friend who was a retired Spanish teacher. The two Minneapolis high school teachers received the biggest grant ($10,000) for creating *Stress Rulz!*, a CD and booklet of English-pronunciation rules in the form of rap music. The other contestants got $8,000 apiece. "It felt wonderful," Emerson says.

Charitable foundations are obligated to give away 5 percent of their assets every year, but when I interviewed Emerson in March 2008, she hadn't figured out what her approach for the year should be. She's been busy. In addition to running the foundation, she manages six rental properties and has a full-time job—as the chief information officer of the Seattle Housing Authority. She hopes that, eventually, she'll be able to convert the foundation into an outright charity and help people directly.

"I always felt that I was going to be called to do something to help others," Emerson says. "When Ray died, I realized that this is what I'm being called to do. I'm carrying on his legacy . . . his life."

FIND LOVE ONLINE

When your mother used to say you needed to "put yourself out there" to find a man, she meant you should try singles night at the bowling alley, or have dinner with somebody's cousin because one date wouldn't kill you. She certainly didn't think you should make yourself available on the web—with your photo, religious affiliation, and likes and dislikes on display for the world to see. But that's only because there was no web.

If you're in the market for love at the beginning of the new millennium, you're crazy not to try an online dating service. Everyone else has. In June 2006, twenty-five million Americans used these sites, and that was in just one month!

There's no question that online dating is efficient. Where else could you "meet" a hundred potential suitors (including some idiots and creeps, unfortunately), and reject most of them without a conversation? How else could you line up twenty dates in a single year? Looking for love is a numbers game: The more you play, the better your chances.

No love connection the first time around? No worries. Just register on a new site, and there'll be a fresh crop of candidates in your inbox in no time. Not in your *real* inbox—these emails go to a special address set up through the site, so any interested parties can't get to you directly without being invited. It's nice to have so much choice and control when it comes to romance, and you can only find that on the web.

"It expands your world," explains my sister's friend Rhonda, who's forty-four. "You can screen them before you even meet them. If you're interested, you move to the phone, then to coffee somewhere."

Note: Many sites charge for their services, and the costs can vary widely. A few sites are free; others claim they are, but then hit you up with hidden charges. Buyer, beware.

Rhonda, a divorced mother of three, wanted a serious relationship with a supportive guy, and if she had to run through a dozen men to find one, she was going to make quick work of it. She had already been out with more than ten men when she got an email on Plentyoffish. com (one of the free sites), from a man whose profile she had never noticed. They spoke on the phone a few times and planned to meet for a drink.

Rhonda expected him to be just another guy to check off the list on her way to finding Mr. Right. But Henry surprised her. He presented her with a little gift—samples from the fragrance company he works for—and something much more valuable: honesty. He told her he'd been married and divorced twice, and had a two-year-old daughter with a woman he'd dated. After that, it was easy.

"The conversation just didn't stop," says Rhonda. "He's very intelligent; he always has a lot to say, but he's not overbearing. A lot of the guys won't listen to what you're saying."

It's been four months, and Rhonda is crazy about Henry. He was very supportive when she had some family issues to resolve, and they've both shut down their online-dating accounts. From here on out, this is just another love story—which is really all it ever was. The Internet element of it is just a means to an end, which is to find love anywhere you can—including the bowling alley.

GO TO
BURNING MAN

More than any other item on The List, this one will strike you as either a living nightmare or a total revelation. But even if it's the last thing on Earth you'd ever want to do, you really should know about Burning Man.

In 1986, in honor of the summer solstice, two guys from San Francisco built a twenty-foot-tall wooden figure on Baker Beach and burned it. Eighteen people watched. That was the first annual Burning Man. Since then, the ritual has moved to Black Rock Desert, Nevada, and grown into a weeklong celebration of art, creative expression, and collaboration. The number of spectators has increased, too—to forty-eight thousand.

For seven days at the end of August, they converge in the desert and create a temporary city—complete with streets, bathrooms, medical centers, and a Division of Mutant Vehicles (more on this later). They sleep in tents, trailers, and trucks, and bring all the supplies they need to survive the week, including tons of water. When it's over, they tear down, pack up, or burn everything they brought, and vanish without a trace.

What happens during that week is hard to explain, but Anna Melillo's story will give you an idea. Melillo, who's fifty-seven, went to Burning Man with a group of friends in 2005. They set up camp in an old prison bus that had been converted into an RV. They also brought scooters, bikes, and a mutant vehicle—a golf cart rigged to play "I Left My Heart in San Francisco" and blow fog from a fog machine—for riding across the hard sand. (People create all kinds of wild vehicles, which have to be approved and registered. For an idea, go to www.burning man.com, click on "Galleries," and type "cupcake" in the search field. You won't believe it.)

> **"You feel thrilled, curious, happy, ebullient. You're just delighted all the time."**
>
> —Anna, age 57

Every year, Burning Man's organizers choose a theme; that year, it was "Psyche." Melillo's camp was on Gestalt Street. Her son and his friends were on nearby Fetish Street. People contributed to the theme in various ways—with art, dance and music performances, costumes, and camps designed to entertain visitors.

"There was a pole-dancing camp and a spanking camp on Fetish Street," Melillo says. "And a goddess camp for women on Ego Street, where straight guys in bathing suits told you how beautiful you are and asked what they could do for you. They shampooed hair and gave manicures, pedicures, and massages."

The art is the main attraction, however. Massive sculptures spring up from the sand—including Burning Man, which is torched on the last night in a wild celebration. "The art installations are the most sensational, outrageous things you've ever seen," says Melillo. "There was a phoenix burning—a block-long steel bird that had fallen to the ground. It was animated; it would move and fire would burst out of it. And that was just one of maybe ninety others. You don't know how they do it."

Equally remarkable is the spirit of generosity and community that pervades the event. Melillo recalls, "You may walk down the street and somebody might offer you blueberries, or you invite them over for pancakes for breakfast. When you go back home, you feel like you went to another planet. You feel very warm and giving, and also sad that the world can't be like that."

PLAN AND PREPARE A SEDUCTION DINNER

If seduction dinners were only about the food, they'd be simple to make. You wouldn't even need to cook. Just stick some grapes, oysters, onions, and walnuts—and any other aphrodisiacs you want—on a platter and call it a night. Oh, and take a bag of M&M's to the bedroom with you (see also "Use Food as Foreplay" on page 176).

But, of course, preparing a meal that entices requires more than that. We use all of our senses to derive pleasure, so if you want to seduce, you've got to make sure things look nice, smell good, feel sensual, taste great, and sound sexy and smooth.

> ## "MORNING-AFTER DINNER WITH CHARLIE"
>
> *Last night you loved the grilled snapper,*
> *How I seasoned it in soy sauce and sesame,*
> *Pungent with ginger, mustard, turmeric so moist*
> *It broke apart on our tongues without chewing.*
>
> *I know how to flavor fish with the touch of my fingers,*
> *Lemons or honey, almonds or garlic, pesto or marinara,*
> *I can control the taste of fish. But last night, after dinner,*
> *I didn't know what to do with my hands.*
>
> —Marilyn Meyer

What you consider seductive dining is a very personal thing, and it's important to remember that, since *you* have to be enticed by this meal, too. There's no point in cooking food for your love interest that does absolutely nothing for you—or, even worse, turns you off. In her new memoir, *It Ain't All About the Cookin'*, celebrity chef Paula Deen describes a scene that would send me screaming from the table, but that works for her—and maybe for you, too:

"If I were going to make a romantic feast today for my man, I'd start with oysters at a table for two at home. A sprinkle of rose petals over the tabletop and a little candlelight wouldn't hurt. Some people say that oysters are an aphrodisiac, and I don't doubt it for a minute. Just think about holding that cold, silky oyster and slipping it down your man's throat. I can't hardly stand it."

Personally, I hate oysters, so there's something to consider: Your seduction dinner may turn into a disappointing meal if you don't know your date's tastes. But to each her own.

Marilyn Meyer is not a celebrity chef, but she is an expert on seduction dinners. Meyer, who just turned sixty, has been divorced for fifteen years—and as a self-described serial monogamist, she's cooked scores of tempting meals. According to Meyer, "What is very seductive is what's inside you and what you're comfortable with. What is not sexy is having a messy kitchen. You need to clean up ahead of time."

With Sinatra crooning in the background, Meyer likes to serve finger appetizers in the kitchen while she finishes preparing dinner. For the meal, she cooks simple yet elegant dishes that don't require a lot of attention at the last minute.

Here's one of her sample menus: salad with wild greens, sliced pear, dried cranberries, roasted pecans or walnuts, and crumbled goat cheese or feta in raspberry vinaigrette; pan-fried trout with sautéed almonds; small red potatoes, roasted with rosemary; and for dessert, fresh strawberries, candied ginger, or dried apricots dipped in dark chocolate.

Always end with chocolate.

QUIT SMOKING

Many women in this book have done things that they describe as liberating. Finally, they're free of the things that limit them: fear, self-doubt, bathing suit tops. But releasing yourself from a dangerous, intractable habit that's plagued you for years is in a league of its own.

Of the many insidious effects of smoking cigarettes—including damaged lungs and stained teeth—guilt is the worst by far. (I know this because I smoked for more than fifteen years.) The guilt, the guilt, the guilt. You know what you're doing is terrible for you, and yet you can't seem to stop it.

You're not alone, of course. Eighteen percent of American women smoke cigarettes, and most will quit many times before they quit for good. By the same token, forty-one million Americans have already kicked the habit. Do they really have something you don't?

I quit the easy way: I got pregnant, for the second time. With my first baby, I was such a nervous wreck that I went straight back to my half-pack-a-day habit the minute she was born. But my second pregnancy was different. The smell of cigarette smoke made me queasy, and after my son was born, I discovered that I had lost my taste for smoking. I just didn't want to do it anymore.

I wish it could be that easy for you, but the struggle to stop smoking is usually long and painful. Some women, like Patti Young, have to push their bodies to the limit before they're able to call it quits. When Young started smoking, in high school, she hid her cigarettes in her sock drawer. When she was in her forties, she hid a chair in the woods behind her house so she could smoke up a storm without her children seeing her.

"I've bummed cigarettes from everyone: the garbage man, people on the street," says Young, who's fifty-one. "And there were many times when I smoked one cigarette and threw the rest of the pack away. I just kept wondering, *When am I ever going to quit? Am I going to get cancer? I just kept dwelling on it, year after year.*"

Then, three years ago, she went on a binge that shocked even her. Young and a friend had rented a cabin in the mountains for a weekend of horseback riding. Young brought the wine—and packs of cigarettes for herself. Her friend didn't smoke.

"It was a beautiful place with no stressors whatsoever," she says. "Yet I sat on the porch and drank three or four glasses of wine . . . and smoked and smoked. I smoked way too much—more than I ever had. I even smoked on horseback. I smoked and smoked and smoked, and then I just had it."

At the end of the weekend, Young threw out the remaining cigarettes. She didn't smoke at all for a while, but when her marriage hit a rough patch, she started up again for one week. That was eighteen months before I interviewed her, and she hasn't picked up a cigarette since. Just thinking about doing it makes her skin crawl, and she starts obsessing: *How bad it is going to be? How bad is it going to taste? If I smoke it, then I'll smell bad. Where am I going to put it?*

"It's just too big," says Young. "It's very much a psychological thing. I'm relieved that I quit. I feel like I finally won the battle."

Done

READ THE CLASSICS

If I told you how many celebrity biographies I've read in my life—including my all-time favorite, Priscilla Presley's *Elvis and Me*—it would be embarrassing. If I told you how many (or, rather, how few) classic novels I've read, it would be mortifying. In high school, I read only what I had to; in college, I didn't take a single literature class. Years ago, when I belonged to a book group, my picks came straight from *People* magazine. Had the group ever voted to read Tolstoy, I probably would have quit. (It wouldn't have mattered, though; the group fell apart soon after we started holding our monthly meetings at a bar.)

How dopey I was.

How dopey I am.

At forty-seven, I remain a literary ignoramus, still operating under the assumption that I'd find classical literature boring and tedious. Isn't it possible, though, that my taste—or at least my tolerance level—has improved over the years? Maybe if I gave Thomas Hardy a chance now, I'd be totally awed, like my friend Peg was when her group chose to read *Far from the Madding Crowd*. She was no fan of the classics before that.

We think we know ourselves so well—our likes, our dislikes, our limits. But when we try something new, we're constantly surprised to see that it suddenly tastes good, or is easier to do, or is actually interesting. It's a little like that Mark Twain quote about his dopey father getting smarter:

> "When I was a boy of fourteen, my father was so ignorant I could hardly stand to have the old man around. But when I got to be

twenty-one, I was astonished at how much he had learned in seven years."

Kathleen, who's forty-seven, had a strong bias against certain classics. In college, she majored in French literature and minored in English literature, and she couldn't stand the nineteenth century. "Everyone was wearing corsets and waiting to get married," she said.

When her book group foisted Jane Austen on her, Kathleen could have been more open-minded about it. After all, many readers adore Austen's satires about the lives and loves of women in nineteenth-century England. Her novels are extremely popular, she's got fan clubs around the world—and she's been dead for nearly two hundred years.

Kathleen cracked her group's selection, *Pride and Prejudice,* with great reluctance. "It was like broccoli at first," she says. "I really had to stop and start a lot. When I started appreciating that Elizabeth Bennett and her sister were analyzing society, I realized the dialogue is witty."

Not witty enough, however, to make Kathleen want to read Austen's *Mansfield Park,* which was next on the group's list. Then one member suggested she see the BBC's production of *Pride and Prejudice,* starring Colin Firth. The sight of Firth, as Mr. Darcy, stripping off for a swim in the lake turned Kathleen around completely.

"Something shifted for me," she says. "I read up on Austen and found that she was the first English writer to write in this form. She was a maverick behind the scenes, helping to change the system."

Kathleen has now read all six of Austen's novels and has seen seven screen adaptations. Lately she's been trying to tackle George Eliot's *Middlemarch,* but it's slow going.

She's a better woman than I am.

BLOW GLASS

What's the matter . . . pottery too easy for you? How about knitting or beading? Why must you go for the craft that involves thrusting a five-foot-long metal pipe into an inferno and pulling out a ball of molten glass that's just a slip away from burning off your hands or feet or both?

Here's why: because that fiery ball is so exquisite, it's worth risking life and limb to create. If you've never seen the process, I suggest you watch "Glass Blowing with Nathaniel Dark and Wildglass.com" on YouTube. The video has three parts; start with part two for instant inspiration. You'll understand the allure.

"I was hooked the second I took my blowpipe, put it in the furnace, and pulled out this white-hot glowing mass," says Melissa Terman, who's forty-six. "It was the combination of awe, indescribable beauty, and danger. I melted as the glass melted."

Terman took her first glass-blowing class at Urban Glass in Brooklyn when she was thirty-eight. At forty she left her career in advertising to pursue her craft full-time. By forty-two, she was a professional glass fuser. "It changed my life," she says. "I never thought I could be an artist, but here I am. I've never been poorer, and I've never been happier."

The complicated process of blowing glass begins in a 2,250-degree furnace, which holds a lake of liquid glass. You open the door, stick in your blowpipe, and turn it to "gather" the glass into a ball. Next, you remove the pipe from the furnace (constantly turning it to keep it centered) and roll the glass over a steel table called a marver to cool it down and shape it. Then you blow air into the pipe to create a bubble in the glass.

To make a bigger piece, you go back to the furnace and gather again. You keep shaping your piece, using a number of tools in addition to the marver. They include:

- Blocks: wooden ladles soaked in water
- Jacks: giant tweezers with two blades
- Newspaper: folded into squares
- Paddles: flat pieces of wood or graphite
- Shears: straight and diamond

"Newspaper is the neatest tool and the simplest tool," says Terman. "It's the closest you get to touching the glass. *The New York Times* is the best. You need four sheets with no color. You fold them up and soak them in water. It becomes a square of eight inches by eight inches."

Once you've finished shaping, you move your glass from the blowpipe to another rod called a punty, and put it into a different kind of furnace called an annealer, where it cools down over a matter of hours or days. The work is intense and physically exhausting. The tools are heavy, the glass is heavy, and it's a million degrees in the studio.

"It's a beautiful kind of tired," says Terman. "You feel accomplished; you feel strong. If you're blowing glass, all you can think about is blowing glass. It's an escape."

If you think about anything else, you're in trouble.

GET A
PILOT'S LICENSE

Long before we had Thelma and Louise, the world was watching Blanche and Louise. Pioneers in the "golden age" of aviation, Blanche Noyes and Louise Thaden were right up there, literally, with Amelia Earhart and Anne Morrow Lindbergh in the pantheon of women pilots. With Noyes as her copilot, Thaden made history as the first woman to win the Bendix Trophy Race, in 1936. She described a mad desire to take to the skies:

"To a psychoanalyst, a woman pilot, particularly a married one with children, must prove an interesting as well as an inexhaustible subject. Torn between two loves, emotionally confused, the desire to fly an incurable disease eating out your life in the slow torture of frustration— she cannot be a simple, natural personality."

Simple? Let's hope not. But wanting to fly shouldn't make you certifiable, either. There were 84,866 student pilots in the United States at the end of 2006, and they couldn't all have been torn up and tortured— at least not by their love of flight.

So what's propelling you to take the pilot's seat? Have you always dreamed of touching the clouds? Or do you suddenly need to grab the controls? That's partly what motivated Jeana Thomas to get her license at age forty. She wasn't having a classic midlife crisis; she was reacting to a very difficult year. After the death of her best friend (who happened to be her ex-husband), Thomas experienced a loss of faith and a sense of dullness in her life. She also developed a growing number of fears, including a fear of flying. What else was there to do but crawl into the cockpit?

Thomas took lessons twice a week after work, and she'd wake up on those mornings with a stomachache that worsened throughout the day. But once she got in the plane and was cruising at six thousand feet above sea level, she was fine.

"I learned that my fear of heights and my fear of flying were two different things," says Thomas, who's fifty-nine. "I wasn't afraid looking down from the airplane, for some reason. The feeling wasn't of power, exactly, or of freedom, but of a higher perspective." And a broader one.

"There's a whole culture up there," she says. "There are roads, highways, and places to turn. Some are identified by landmarks on the ground, others by instruments. It quickly made me have a stereoscopic experience of the area, and of the earth in general. Even when I was driving on the highway, I would be aware of my progress as if I was seeing it from above. It was fascinating. I love knowing all that."

The learning curve was steep for Thomas, but it was like anything else: Once she got the hang of it, flying was easy. "My body seemed to pick it up before my brain did. I knew what to do with my hands and feet before I could explain to you why I did it."

Thomas got her license six months later, and while she never became an avid pilot, the experience marked a clear turning point in her life. "So many gifts were returned to me," she says. "Now, almost twenty years later, I feel younger, prettier, more confident, and more alive than I did in my thirties."

Pretty valuable lessons.

89

Done

SPEND
TWENTY-FOUR
HOURS IN BED

The dictionary definition of the word "decadence" doesn't nearly do it justice. Instead of "lack of moral and intellectual discipline" and "luxurious self-indulgence," the entry should read: "Lily Signature Canvas Satchel by Coach" and "entire family-size bag of Doritos." There's a secondary definition I'd like to add—"stay in bed all day"—but I'm afraid it wouldn't make it in. This one is so decadent, it's almost unmentionable.

Here are some reasons why you could never, ever do it:

- You have a job, for goodness' sake.
- You have kids to take care of.
- You've got a dentist/haircut/therapy appointment.
- You don't have enough time as it is.
- You'd feel guilty.
- What would everyone think?
- You wouldn't be able to enjoy it.

Really? Which of the following isn't enjoyable? Sleeping late. Drinking coffee in bed. Actually reading the newspaper. Eating toast, with butter and jam, in bed (screw the crumbs). Starting a good book. Watching a bad movie. Eating peanut butter off a spoon. Painting your toenails. Napping. Watching *Law & Order* reruns. Snacking in bed (Doritos?). Reading *People* and *Us Weekly*. Watching *What Not to Wear* (see "Hire a Personal Shopper" on page 110). Not moving a muscle for anyone or anything.

Clearly, this scenario requires that you exile your partner and children for twelve hours or more. You can invite your mate to stay in bed with you if you really want to, but it's a different kind of day than the one I'm talking about. To me, staying in bed isn't about catching up on sex, or bonding with your mate, or making a political statement in front of hordes of reporters. Those things take effort. Spending the day in bed is about doing nothing, for no good reason, and feeling entitled to do it.

Think back to your twenties, when you'd stay out all night and sleep all day. I don't know about you, but I didn't think twice about waking up after noon and lying around until it was time to go out again—at eight, nine, or ten at night. It didn't matter whether it was thirty degrees and snowing outside or eighty degrees and sunny—I felt no need to get out and be productive. In fact, I'm not sure it even crossed my mind. Now *that's* luxury.

That person, the one who could ignore the clock, is far removed from this person, the one who stuffs ham sandwiches into paper bags every morning at seven fifteen. The one who walks the dog at seven forty and is back in the house, coffee and computer in hand, by eight. But I still have memories.

When I was in college, I visited my sister at Emory University in Atlanta for a long weekend. There was a fraternity formal that Saturday night, and she fixed me up with a date, a very sweet guy named Buford. My sister and I had such a jolly good time that we couldn't get up in the morning . . . so we didn't get up at all. We stayed in her dorm room all day, watching TV, eating bologna sandwiches, and talking. We saw a rerun of an ABC Movie of the Week from the '70s called *Say Goodbye, Maggie Cole,* starring Susan Hayward as a widowed doctor who goes to work in an inner-city clinic—a film so cheesy and memorable, we still refer to it.

I'd give anything to have another day like that with my sister. I could, too.

lost 47 lbs

LOSE FIFTY-PLUS
POUNDS

She's a new woman. That's what people say when you quit work and are happy for a change, or when you win the lottery and start tipping 20 percent instead of your usual, miserable 10.

I feel like a new woman. That's what you say after you lose a ton of weight and find yourself with more energy, enthusiasm, and self-confidence than you've had in years.

As anyone with three sizes of jeans in their drawer can tell you, losing weight is an epic battle—on the same scale as giving up smoking (see page 186). Forty-five million Americans diet each year; the majority of them don't lose a pound. And at least 95 percent of those who do lose weight gain back most or all of it within two years.

Not great odds. Still, it's better to have lost and gained back than to never have lost at all. Having triumphed once, you may be more inclined to try again.

When Jane Corwin lost eighty pounds in her mid-thirties, it changed her life—she became an avid cyclist. When she regained much of the weight in her early forties, she couldn't keep up with her regular riding group anymore. Corwin wouldn't accept that; she had lost the weight once before, and she was going to lose it again.

The tipping point the first time was when Corwin reached two hundred pounds and couldn't fit into a size 16 anymore. "That's what shook me—having to go to the plus-size department," she says. So she came up with her own diet: nothing for breakfast (only one cup of coffee with nonfat cream); Slim-Fast or Lean Cuisine for lunch; and a low-calorie, low-fat dinner. Her husband was at home then, and he cooked a recipe from *Cooking Light* magazine every night.

For exercise, Corwin dragged an old Huffy bike from the garage. She started at two miles and worked her way up to twenty, buying a $400 bike along the way. Between riding and dieting, she went from 200 pounds to 118 in less than a year. (She then decided she was too thin, and increased her weight to a more natural 130.)

"I was a different person that fall," says Corwin, who's forty-six. "I don't think you feel it as you're doing it, but when you look at before-and-after pictures, boy, it feels great to admire yourself and not say, 'Don't look at that picture.'"

Corwin became a serious cyclist, joined a group of high-level riders, and traded up to a $1,200 bike. But when she lost her job in a round of layoffs and had a long commute to her new job, she suddenly had no time to ride. Her husband was working again, too, and he had no time to cook. Corwin starting eating too much of the wrong foods, and the pounds piled back on.

In 2005, Corwin found a job closer to home. She started biking again, but she couldn't match the pace of her former group. And even though she was exercising, she didn't lose the weight that was holding her back. So, in 2007, she went back on the diet that had worked so well a decade earlier. After six months, Corwin had lost thirty-five pounds.

Now she rides a $4,000 bike.

90. LOSE FIFTY-PLUS POUNDS

Retired!

TAKE A YEAR OFF

You can read this and weep, or you can start making plans. Your choice.

In 2004, Libbie Stellas took her daughter—her only child—to look at colleges. Somewhere between Kenyon in Ohio and Bryn Mawr in Pennsylvania, Stellas, who is fifty-four, began wishing for a do-over—a chance to head back out into the world and find herself.

Two years later, Stellas was emptying her God Box, in which she leaves her worries behind on pieces of paper for God to work on, when she found one that read: "I don't know what to do about this desire to get in my car and go." She took stock of her situation: She hated her job as a nonprofit fundraiser; she hadn't had a man in her life for years; and she lived in an empty nest. What was stopping her?

"Something in my life had to change, because something already was changing," she says. "I was working with seniors who were moving from their homes into assisted living, and I saw a future I didn't want to have. They didn't want to let go of things. They were frightened to make a move. The only way I was going to be more flexible at eighty was to be more flexible now."

Stellas quit her job and started doing gardening work. She considered the Peace Corps (see page 150) and other volunteer projects, but really, she just wanted to hit the road for a year. So she bought a Ford Focus station wagon and made plans to leave in the spring.

Stellas had lived the first half her life on the East Coast, and the second half in Seattle. Maybe during her travels, she'd figure out where to spend the rest of it. She rented out her house and shed most of her belongings. The one thing she took with her was a box filled with forty-one diaries dating back to sixth grade. She would read them all on her trip, clipping parts that she wanted to keep and throwing out the rest.

She drove from Seattle to Las Vegas to Bisbee, Arizona, where she stayed for a week to see if it had potential. (Nice place, but too brown.) She drove east to the outskirts of New Orleans to visit a friend she hadn't seen in twenty-nine years, and then north to New Jersey for her thirty-fifth high school reunion in May. She spent the summer there, at her sister's house, visiting old boyfriends, eating sweet Jersey tomatoes, and wondering if it was time to move back East. But she was too much of a West Coast person now.

Stellas's daughter flew to New Jersey at the end of the summer so the two of them could drive back across the country together. "We talked about men and liberation, and what mattered to her, and how she might make career decisions," says Stellas. "It was fabulous."

All told, Stellas lived out of suitcases for only nine months; she ran out of money before the full year was up. She went to house sit in Maui for three weeks, and then returned to Seattle and house sat there. Even though she had to cut her trip short, she discovered something important on the road: she wanted to remain in Seattle.

"I think I have another love in me," she says, "and traveling around the country isn't the best way to make that happen. Who I spend my life with is more important than where I spend my life, and I have twenty-two years of a very broad and deep community here. I still have a lot to do that I want to do here."

HAVE A BABY LATE IN LIFE

Having a baby is a shake-up at any age, but having one after forty can be seismic. A new baby, whether it's a long-awaited first or an accidental fourth, means a brand-new life for you—one filled with stuff and mess and exhaustion. Are you really up for that? You already have trouble staying awake past midnight, and if you've had a glass or two of wine, forget it—you're gone by ten.

Maybe you do have less energy than you used to. So what? One hundred thousand American women over age forty give birth each year. When was the last time you heard one of them say, "It's the worst thing I've ever done. Having that baby keeps me old"?

The birth rate for women between ages forty and forty-four has tripled in the last twenty-five years, and it's a nonevent to see a mother with gray-streaked hair pushing a stroller. If you have any doubt about that, just go to the playground sometime and check out the range of women sitting on benches, holding sippy cups. The age span is huge, and the math is ridiculous. It's like one of those word problems about the moving trains:

I'm forty-six, and my youngest child, William, is twelve. His best friend's mother, LeAnne, is forty, and her youngest is one. When her baby starts kindergarten, my baby will be a high school sophomore. I'll be an empty-nester at fifty-two; she won't be one until she's fifty-eight, even though she started having children three years earlier than I did.

Then there's Caroline Leavitt, who was forty-four when she had her first and only child (and she was always the youngest woman in her obstetrician's waiting room). She won't have any peace and quiet in her house until she's sixty-one—and she couldn't be happier about it.

Leavitt never wanted children (she was too much a free spirit to be tied down), and she made that clear to all of her boyfriends, including her future husband. He banked on her changing her mind—which she did, overnight, in her late thirties.

"It wasn't subtle . . . it was like a sledgehammer," she says. "I went from 'Kids are not for me' to 'I *really* want a baby.' It was a very physical want—consistent and unrelenting. There was no way I was going to live without it."

Leavitt had many early miscarriages, and then she had a devastating one when she was three and a half months pregnant. Her doctor wanted her to start thinking about egg donation or adoption, but somehow Leavitt knew she would have her own baby. A few months after the last miscarriage, she was pregnant again—and this one stuck.

"It was like the second coming; it was incredible," she says. "I was so happy. My obstetrician always liked seeing me because I never complained. I loved having morning sickness. I felt like having a baby was absolutely the right thing to do."

Now Leavitt has a house crawling with kids—her son and his friends. "I love having them here," she says. "I'm like the house mom." If she had started earlier, she would have had more children; in fact, she and her husband tried to adopt when their son was two. But if she had started *much* earlier, she would have regretted it. So Leavitt is content with the way things turned out, even though she's an older mother.

"We have friends in their fifties whose kids are in college," she says. "It's very different for us. But having a baby when you're older really keeps you young."

LIVE WITH LESS

Watch me hyperventilate while I take stock of my life. Here's a fraction of the senseless and annoying stuff I've accumulated and can't seem to dispose of:

- Ten stacks of old bank statements with rubber bands around them
- Two velvet dresses, one taffeta party skirt, two pairs of black pants, and one silk suit, not worn in years
- Three sets of good china
- A basket of old pocketbooks, and another of old hats
- A pile of empty picture frames
- More dishtowels, mugs, serving bowls, decorative pieces, and sandals than I have places to store them

This is why I can't wait to retire and downsize to an apartment—I won't have room for pictureless frames and china service for forty.

I'm more than a little envious of my friend Louise, who, as soon as her nest emptied out, sold her house in New York and moved to a three-bedroom condo in Los Angeles, taking with her only the things that she really needed or loved (see "Make a Big Move" on page 112). I'm jealous that she lives a block from the beach and can smell the ocean every day, and that she's able to travel so light.

It's not just the material stuff that weighs you down. If it feels good to clean out the hall closet every year, imagine the joy of eliminating meaningless pursuits and time-draining distractions from your life—things like unfulfilling jobs, unhappy relationships, and unwanted obligations. Maybe if you got rid of the baggage, you could figure out exactly what is important to you. Or maybe it's the other way around—once you figure out what's important, you'll drop those bags and run.

Suzy Sands knows what she wants to do with her life: turn her part-time landscaping business into her full-time job (see "Start Your Own Business" on page 104). Right now, though, she's got an art director job at a magazine that's too good to leave. When she retires, she'll make whatever adjustments she needs to pursue her dream—including downsizing her life.

"What is 'enough' is subjective," says Sands. "I try to imagine living light: I'll drive a little Scion; it costs under $20,000. I used to like to wear designer clothes, but it's not at the top of my list anymore. I don't want to be acquisitive."

Lynne Macco has already pared her life down to its bare necessities. She and her husband retired early and spent the summer of 2008 being lighthouse keepers in Maine. (For more on her various adventures, see "Play in the Snow" on page 140.) They'd already sold their house and moved into a rental—and then they moved out of that. They rented storage space and sorted through their things, figuring out what they absolutely couldn't part with, because their escapades didn't end when summer did. They plan to spend seven months in a rented beach house and then take their boat to the Bahamas in April 2009.

"I'm getting rid of extra clothing," Macco says. "I'm looking around and saying, 'What do I have that I don't really need?' I'm keeping china from my grandmother, and our bedroom and a guest bedroom's worth of furniture. We both agreed not to judge what the other one keeps.

"When I got divorced, I left with five pieces of furniture. There's something very healthy about getting rid of stuff, very freeing."

I'm all for that.

MOUNT AN
ART EXHIBIT

Putting on an art exhibit causes the same anxiety as throwing a lavish party: *What if nobody comes? What if everyone comes late and leaves early? What if the food stinks or the champagne runs out?* And, worst of all: *What if they think I'm a loser?* But showing your work presents an added worry: *What if they don't get it?*

Being understood is a basic human want. Imagine sharing your innermost thoughts with a friend over nonfat lattes and having her go, "Huh?" Now imagine creating a piece of art that makes no sense to anybody else. Every artist, from Cassatt to O'Keeffe to Leibovitz, uses her work as a means of self-expression—a way to reveal a hidden quality, a secret passion, or a deep belief. The idea of exposing yourself and having people stare blankly is painful—and terrifying. But what if they smile and nod their heads in recognition of whatever thought, hope, or truth you're hoping to convey? What if they really connect?

Only one way to find out.

Cathy Dalton, an avid photographer, decided it was a chance worth taking. Dalton, who's fifty-four, had started traveling extensively in her late forties, primarily to feed her passion for photography. After two trips to India, she began to put an exhibit together in her mind, spurred by friends and a personal desire to put herself out there.

"I felt compelled to share my experiences, at the risk of being very vulnerable," she says. "I just was excited to share a creative outlet that I had discovered and felt good about."

Dalton had plenty to work with: She'd taken more than two thousand photos over her two visits. As she went through them, she saw a collection of different, yet similar, expressions of emotion and experience. "The selections were partly planned, but mostly they presented themselves," she says. "They spoke to me." In the end, she chose twenty-eight photos to display.

Finding the venue was surprisingly easy. A new yoga studio was opening in a nearby town, and Dalton asked her own yoga teacher for the owner's name. She made the call, set up a meeting, and pulled together some samples. The next thing she knew, she had a gallery opening to deal with—in six weeks.

"I was excited but overwhelmed to realize how much work it was going to take—printing the photos, having them mounted, figuring out how I wanted to hang them, paying for them. This was about people that I love, experiences that I love, and creating an environment. It was exposing part of myself to my friends, who had never seen that side of me. It was very, very big."

Around one hundred people saw Dalton's work over the course of the evening. By the end, she felt validated: Her work is good, and people really got it. "It was gratifying how many people said, 'Wow, I really want to go to India.'"

94. MOUNT AN ART EXHIBIT

FIND RELIGION

When some women find their lives lacking, they change their circumstances. They switch careers or leave their marriage or make a big move (see pages 126, 102, and 112, respectively). But that may not be enough for you—not if you're looking for a deeper transformation. If the void in your life is one of spirit and soul, you've really got to fill it with faith.

Americans are in flux when it comes to religion, according to a 2008 study by The Pew Forum on Religion & Public Life. The study shows that 28 percent of American adults have switched faiths (or dropped out altogether).

Perhaps you're also looking for a new flock to join—and even if you're not religious, you may be seeking a spiritual connection outside of formal religion. What's leading you to search for meaning at this stage of your life? Are you simply dissatisfied, or has something major—an event beyond your control—occurred and punched holes in your beliefs and expectations? That's what happened to Robin Bradford in the aftermath of Hurricane Katrina. She didn't know how to live with the things she had seen.

Bradford, who's forty-five, works as a development director for a nonprofit group in Austin, Texas, that builds low-income housing. When the hurricane hit, she and her colleagues sprang into action to deal with the influx of victims. She helped to manage volunteers and set up food pantries; she also decided to collect the stories of survivors to solicit money from donors.

The first two months were very rewarding; the families were grateful, and the outpouring of generosity was inspiring. But then something shifted for Bradford as she began to realize that the problems the flood victims faced—and had brought with them—were impossible to fix.

"No single community can change generational poverty and illiteracy," Bradford says. "You read all this stuff about poverty, but it's not the same as sitting in someone's living room and seeing it. I was just overwhelmed by the number of young women I met who looked like they were fourteen, carrying their new baby. Or the babies with shunts in their heads who were born prematurely to mothers who are drug addicts."

Bradford suddenly couldn't sleep at night. "Somewhere in there, I had a kind of spiritual crisis. All the different religious teachings I had had rushed through my head: what Jesus said about the poor, and how Buddhism says that suffering is the human condition."

Something about that philosophy worked for Bradford. She started studying Buddhism and discovered that it really isn't about faith; it's about acceptance. "The first teaching is that human life basically sucks, and that we always have a sense of dissatisfaction," she says. "The second truth is that there's a way to contain that feeling of suffering, which is by releasing one's expectations and desires, and letting things be as they are."

For Bradford, that meant stepping back from her involvement with evacuees—and with one family in particular—and not rushing in to fix things. She didn't see the family for six months. When the grandmother had a stroke, Bradford waited a few days before visiting her in the hospital and spent that time thinking about what the woman really needed. Bradford decided on something simple: homemade chicken soup for dinner, served in china bowls with proper silverware. And when she took it to the hospital, she went as a friend, not a volunteer.

BUNGEE JUMP

xplain this to me: Why on earth would you or anybody else attach a stretchy cord to your ankles and do a swan dive off a bridge? I understand that people are waiting below in a boat, ready to pull you in and ferry you to shore. But that's after you've plummeted a hundred feet or more—hanging upside down. Call me a scaredy-cat (you wouldn't be wrong), but this seems even crazier than skydiving (see "Skydive" on page 116). At least there, you're right-side up.

Doing a headfirst freefall obviously appeals to somebody, because bungee jumping is available in at least ten states in this country. As extreme sports go, it's relatively cheap (about $100 a jump) and easy. You don't need any training or equipment, and sometimes you can show up at the jump zone without an appointment and just do it. If you think it's a thrill you'd like to seek, here's what you can expect the first time you jump:

When you get to the site—whether it's a bridge, building, or crane—jump operators will set you up with a body harness that attaches to a set of bungee cords. (Some outfits still use a simple ankle attachment, but accidents over the years have made commercial operators move toward harnesses.) The cords hook into webbing that's bound around the structure you're jumping from. As you dive, the cords stretch to about twice their normal length and then contract, cushioning your fall and pulling you upward again.

Ann Curry of the *Today* show told 5.8 million viewers how bungee jumping feels—while she was actually doing it. On December 17, 2007,

Curry jumped 120 feet off the Transporter Bridge in Middlesbrough, England, to raise money for the United Way and Save the Children. It was such an event that Tom Hanks flew to New York from Los Angeles so he could offer commentary along with Al Roker, Meredith Vieira, and David Gregory.

Even though she was going to be caught by her ankles, Curry wore two body harnesses for safety. James, the operator, told her to put her tiptoes on the edge of the platform and to keep focusing on the horizon. Now, the countdown: "Four, three, two, one . . . bungee!" And off Curry went, in perfect swan form. As she hurtled toward the River Tees, here's what she said:

"Oh, my good lord! Oh, my good lord, this is fantastic. Yay! Oh, my good lord. Oh, this is fantastic. I recommend it, actually. Hey, guys, this is actually fun.

"I feel all the blood in my body in my brain. I feel actually like a bird. That first moment, when you're first falling, you do have your life flash before your eyes.

"I can really say that this is very relaxing. They're going to be lowering me now, soon, into a boat. The world upside down is really kind of beautiful. You know what? This wasn't as scary as I thought it would be."

As they lowered her into the boat, Curry grabbed the hands of one of the operators. He told her to look up at her toes so she could bend and come in butt-first. And when she was finally sitting down, she said, "The world is right again."

Tom Hanks gave her a 9.8.

gone

SLEEP WITH A YOUNGER MAN

You can buy all the age-defying creams you want. You can glaze your hair, tone your abs, and borrow your daughter's clothes. But if you really want to feel young and sexy, try sleeping with a man who can't remember the first lunar landing.

You'd think it would be the other way around—that being with someone a decade or more younger than you would just emphasize your advanced age and make you depressed. It's certainly not a confidence booster when your lover says things like, "Did you have color television back then?" But the power of attracting someone who really *is* young and sexy is worth the occasional moment of self-doubt.

While the conquest is a thrill, there's an even bigger draw to sleeping with a younger man: It's fun! You get to have sex with someone who has energy, enthusiasm, and a proverbial tiger in his tank (he may not remember that one, either), and recapture your own youthfulness while you're at it.

> **"It felt illicit. It was very, very exciting. Did I feel deserving? I felt like hot stuff."**
>
> —Nancy, age 50

When you're with a younger man, you do things you haven't thought about doing in years—and not just in bed. That's because younger men have lives. They go to clubs. They stay out late. They eat at trendy restaurants. If you spend any amount of time together, you'll have a life, too. It's not that you couldn't do those things with a man your own age—it's that you don't.

Five years before Demi met Ashton, and two years before Madonna met Guy, Nancy, a single, forty-year-old mother of two, started a relationship with a man twelve years her junior. A decade later, she still recalls the first time they slept together.

"It felt illicit," Nancy says. "He was young . . . and we were on the floor! It was very, very exciting. It brought out the sex kitten in me that didn't exist before. Did I feel deserving? I thought I was hot stuff. It was all fun, because you're riding a little bit of a fantasy. Everything was just for kicks. I would wear a leather skirt that I wouldn't have put on otherwise. I was enjoying things I probably would have given up."

Happily, many women are discovering their inner kitten through reverse May–December romances. In a 2003 study by the AARP, 34 percent of women over forty said they were dating younger men, and 35 percent of them preferred it to dating older men. See? It's not just for celebrities anymore.

It's hard to separate the chicken from the egg in this new dating trend. Are you attractive to young men because you're hot? Or are you hot because you have a young lover? Who cares? If sleeping with a man who's ten years younger makes *you* feel ten years younger, run with it. Nancy did, and she's been married to her "conquest" for four years. She's fifty now, and he's thirty-eight.

Works for her!

BUY A NEGLIGEE

There are two types of women in this world: those who wear silky negligees, and those who wear flannel pajamas with piggies on them. I'm the piggy type. But I've always wished I were sophisticated enough to pull off a full-length peignoir, like Myrna Loy does in *The Thin Man* or Katharine Hepburn does in *Bringing Up Baby*.

Lately I've been thinking, *Maybe this is a case of "If you wear it, it will come."* Perhaps if I bought a negligee, I'd feel like a sexy sophisticate. So last week, when I took my daughter Madeline dress shopping for her cousin's graduation, I dragged her up to the Intimates department at Nordstrom. She's fifteen and not too mortified to dig through a sales rounder of peekaboo nighties, looking for something decent for her mother to wear. I was the embarrassed one; she was yanking things off the bar left and right.

First, let me say how shocked I was to discover that even at an upscale department store, everything is polyester. There wasn't a single silk item on the floor. Nor were there many long negligees, or ones with matching robes. I tried to picture Myrna Loy in a shiny synthetic nightie that stopped halfway up her thighs. Couldn't do it.

The saleswoman asked me if I was looking for a bridal set; apparently, there's only one occasion that merits looking elegant in the bedroom. She pulled the only set they had and led us to the dressing room. Between the three of us, we had grabbed nearly a dozen negligees.

I wasn't sure what I'd see in the mirror, and I was truly excited to find out. (If you are a longtime negligee wearer, this may seem dopey to you, but when you're doing it for the first time at forty-six, it's a big deal.) Some of the negligees were absurd, like the gauzy banana-yellow one with the matching thong. But some looked quite nice. They didn't cling too much, and they created the illusion of cleavage where there wasn't any.

The one I thought looked stupidest on the hanger actually looked best on me. It was a short, pale pink froufrou number by Oscar de la Renta, with skinny black straps and black polka-dot tulle over the boobs. I saved the bridal set for last, primarily because it cost $460 (for *polyester!*), but also because it was exactly what I had in mind.

It was sophisticated. It fit perfectly, and I felt beautiful in it. The V-neck top was almost all lace, but it was designed so that you couldn't see my nipples. The lace dipped down but stopped just above the pubic bone. The rest was an ivory satin that fell straight to the floor. I liked how it looked on me—or rather, how I looked in it—so much that I didn't feel like a fraud.

I bought the pink de la Renta, which was $40, marked down from $68. I thought my husband might laugh at it, but he said it was "enticing." I wore it twice, marveling at how comfortable it was. But the other day, I caught a glimpse of the tag. It was a size extra-large that someone had stuck in the section for mediums. Now I know why it barely touched my skin.

Suddenly, because it's two sizes too big, I don't like it anymore. I won't wear it again. But the next time there's a sale in the negligee department, I'll go.

BLOW OFF
THE DAY

The other night, my fifteen-year-old daughter made a passing reference to Ferris Bueller, jokingly turning the name into a verb, as in "I totally Ferris Buellered yesterday, and nobody caught me." The 1986 movie *Ferris Bueller's Day Off*, which stars Matthew Broderick as a fun-loving high school truant, came out eight years before my daughter was born, and she's never seen it. Yet even for her, it's shorthand for blowing off all responsibility, thumbing your nose at authority, and playing hooky from everyday life.

Sounds good, doesn't it? Better than it did in high school, frankly, when you risked losing phone and driving privileges if your parents found out. Who's going to ground you now if you call in sick or skip the fundraising meeting? When you Ferris Bueller as an adult, nothing is hanging over your head.

Two other shake-ups in this book might seem similar to this one: "Escape," on page 134, and "Spend Twenty-Four Hours in Bed," on page 194. But blowing off the day has one key distinguishing element: It involves deception or delinquency, or both. That's the exciting part! There's something you should be doing—that other people *expect* you to do—and you just say screw it.

In a way, blowing off the day is like stealing: You're taking time away from an obligation and using it for your own enjoyment. Skipping out isn't just escaping from the everyday; it's pursuing something you really enjoy. Maybe you want to plant your vegetable garden when the sun is shining and nobody else is around. Or take in two matinees and a big tub of popcorn on a cold, rainy day. Beats organizing files.

It's been a while since I've blown off a day, but the last time I did, it was doubly terrific because I was ignoring a ton of work. I'd been writing around the clock for three months, and even though I wasn't finished with my project, I gave myself a break. The week before Christmas, I organized an outing for the women on my block, all close friends. Seven of us squeezed into a minivan and drove forty-five minutes to the Italian section of the Bronx for an afternoon of shopping and eating. My editor couldn't have reached me if she tried, and on that particular day, I couldn't have cared less.

Because she's a self-described type A personality, Patti Young, a teacher, would never have done that. She needs ideal conditions, including a light load at school, if she's going to ditch work for a day. For Young, who's fifty-one, the weather has to be perfect as well—one of those golden spring days that come along only a few times a year. When everything lines up just right, she'll call in sick and take her horse up into the mountains for the day.

"I've worked for the public school system for twenty-five years," Young says. "They owe me a day. I have a fortune invested in my horses, and I rarely get to ride. When you're seventy, do you look back and think, *I should have worked more?* Forget it!"

MAKE YOUR OWN LIST

I hope the ninety-nine adventures in *The List*—and the stories of the women who've been changed by them—inspire you to finally pursue the windsurfing/forestry/African dance class that's captured your imagination. It's never too late to start your own list . . . and why wait a minute longer?

- _____

- _____

- _____

- _____

- _____

- _____

- _____

- _____

- _____

- _____

- _____
- _____
- _____
- _____
- _____
- _____
- _____
- _____
- _____
- _____
- _____
- _____
- _____
- _____
- _____
- _____

100. MAKE YOUR OWN LIST

ACKNOWLEDGMENTS

I've got many wonderful people to thank for their support, which makes me a very lucky woman. Here they are:

- My children, Madeline and William, who put up with an absentee (and often cranky) mom for five months
- My husband, Julian, who filled the void without blinking
- My family and friends, who never stopped asking how it was going (even if they wanted to)
- My agent, Matthew Elblonk, who wouldn't let this one go
- My editor, Brooke Warner, who saw what *The List* could and should be
- The daring, fun, and gutsy women who shared their stories of discovery (and got their friends to share, too)

The List has been one of the best shake-ups of my life, and it couldn't have happened without you. So thanks!

ABOUT THE
AUTHOR

Gail Belsky is a writer, editor, and adjunct professor of journalism at Fordham University. She is also the editor of the essay collection *Over the Hill and Between the Sheets* (Springboard Press, 2007). Belsky lives in New Jersey with her husband and two children.

SELECTED TITLES FROM SEAL PRESS

For more than thirty years,
Seal Press has published groundbreaking books.
By women. For women.
Visit our website at www.sealpress.com.
Check out the Seal Press blog at www.sealpress.com/blog.

Tango: An Argentine Love Story, by Camille Cusumano. $15.95, 1-58005-250-9. The spicy travel memoir of a woman who left behind a failed fifteen-year relationship and fell in love with Argentina through the dance that embodies intensity, freedom, and passion.

For Keeps: Women Tell the Truth About Their Bodies, Growing Older, and Acceptance, edited by Victoria Zackheim. $15.95, 1-58005-204-5. This inspirational collection of personal essays explores the relationship that aging women have with their bodies.

Above Us Only Sky, by Marion Winik. $14.95, 1-58005-144-8. A witty and engaging book from NPR commentator Marion Winik about facing midlife without getting tangled up in the past or hung up on the future.

Go Your Own Way: Women Travel the World Solo, edited by Faith Conlon, Ingrid Emerick & Christina Henry de Tessan. $15.95, 1-58005-199-5. Paying tribute to the empowerment of independent adventure and discovery, women recount the thrills of traveling solo, from Borneo and Senegal to Argentina, Paris, Japan, and more.

The Nonrunner's Marathon Guide for Women: Get Off Your Butt and On with Your Training, by Dawn Dais. $14.95, 1-58005-205-3. Cheer on your inner runner with this accessible, funny, and practical guide.

Women Who Run, by Shanti Sosienski. $15.95, 1-58005-183-9. An inspirational and informative book profiling twenty very different women and exploring what drives them to run.